西方旅行文学作品选读

——以中国形象为视角

朱江勇　江利华　钟　俊◎主编

合肥工業大學出版社

图书在版编目(CIP)数据

西方旅行文学作品选读:以中国形象为视角/朱江勇,江利华,钟俊主编.—合肥:合肥工业大学出版社,2018.5
ISBN 978-7-5650-3806-8

Ⅰ.①西… Ⅱ.①朱…②江…③钟… Ⅲ.①英语—阅读教学—高等学校—教材 Ⅳ.①H319.37

中国版本图书馆CIP数据核字(2017)第329411号

西方旅行文学作品选读
——以中国形象为视角

朱江勇 江利华 钟 俊 主编　　责任编辑 王钱超

出 版	合肥工业大学出版社	版 次	2018年5月第1版
地 址	合肥市屯溪路193号	印 次	2018年7月第1次印刷
邮 编	230009	开 本	710毫米×1010毫米 1/16
电 话	总 编 室:0551-62903038	印 张	11
	市场营销部:0551-62903198	字 数	180千字
网 址	www.hfutpress.com.cn	印 刷	合肥现代印务有限公司
E-mail	hfutpress@163.com	发 行	全国新华书店

ISBN 978-7-5650-3806-8　　定价:39.00元

如果有影响阅读的印装质量问题,请与出版社市场营销部联系调换。

◎国家旅游局“2015 年旅游业青年专家培养计划人选”结题成果◎

◎桂林旅游学院外国语言学及其应用语言学学科建设特色课程◎

编委会

主　编

朱江勇　（桂林旅游学院　博士、教授）

江利华　（桂林旅游学院　硕士、副教授）

钟　俊　（厦门医学院　博士、副教授）

副主编

黄晓萍　（桂林旅游学院　外国语学院院长、教授）

陆礼春　（桂林旅游学院　博士、副教授）

涂运根　（桂林旅游学院　博士、讲师）

序

朱江勇教授、江利华副教授和钟俊博士主编的教材《西方旅行文学作品选读——以中国形象为视角》即将付梓，嘱我作序，既感荣幸，又觉惶恐，但盛情难却，权写几点读后感。

朱江勇教授任职于桂林旅游学院，是国家旅游局授予的旅游业青年专家。他领衔主编的这部教材，适应国家旅游业的发展和所在高校的教学需要，从西方旅行文学作品入手，将学术性较强的中国形象这个话题引入旅游英语专业本科教学，这是一种很有创意的可贵探索，对学生语言能力、文化能力和翻译能力的培养都有积极作用。

首先，该教材有助于提高学生的读写能力。对外语专业学生，包括旅游英语专业学生而言，语言能力是将来从事与外语相关行业不可或缺的技能。如何形成外语能力，如何提高外语能力？诸多外语界前辈用亲身经历告诉我们，必须大量阅读外语文学作品，而旅游英语专业的同学除了阅读一般性英语文学作品外，还要经常接触英语旅行文学作品，只有这样才能深切感受该类作品的魅力，提高自身旅游英语阅读与表达能力。

其次，该教材有助于提高学生的文化能力。现在是全球化时代，国际交流日益频繁，文化能力或跨文化能力是优秀人才的一笔重要财富。中国是一个多民族国家，汉族和各少数民族文化特色鲜明，桂林所在的广西地区本身就是一个以壮族文化为主体的亚文化区。世界更是一个文化多元、价值观各异的大千世界。要想推动世界和平发展，每个合格的世界公民都有责任热爱、发扬和推广自己国家和地区的文化，尊重、理解和善待其他国家和地区的文化。前面所说的语言能力不能狭义地理解为就语言谈语言，而应该从广义上理解为在跨文化交际背景下恰当使用语言进行文化交流的能力。否则，我们跟外国人交流，语音语调再漂亮，词汇量再大，语法意识再强，终不能达到有效沟通的效果。所以，当代旅游英语专业大学生要力争将语言学习与文化学习结合起来，具有国际视野，增强文化意识，方能成为一个真正的"文化人"。

再次,该教材有助于提高学生的翻译能力。教材选取13至20世纪西方旅行文学中有代表性的十四个文本,从历史、地理、社会、政治、外交、民俗等多方面展示了西方人眼中一个动态的中国形象。作者的经历不同,立场各异,跟中国的感情有远有近,对中国自然景观和风土人情的描述各有偏好与侧重。但是,有一点是共同的,这些作者都是从世界看中国。阅读这些作品,我们可以从中分析和领悟外国人是如何用英语描写中国、展示中国、评论中国。在中国文化"走出去"的当代大潮中,通过西方旅行文学作品了解西方人的思维特点及用语习惯,去粗取精,为我所用,有利于我们在"走出去"的翻译活动中,用西方人喜闻乐见的方式讲好中国故事。只有这样,我们的对外传播与翻译作品才能真正受到外国听众和读者的青睐,不仅能"走出去",而且能"走进去",深入西方读者的内心,达到良好的跨文化交际目的,为中国文化融入世界、促进世界文明发展贡献力量。

培养优秀的旅游英语专业人才不是一件容易的事。朱江勇教授和同事在教材编写和课程改革上做了一件有意义的开拓性的工作。以该教材为契机,他们似乎还可以进一步拓展,开发相关教材和课程,比如英语旅行散文、英语旅行诗歌、中英旅行文学作品对比与赏析等,在提高学生语言能力的同时,培养其文化素养及思辨能力,助力中国旅游业的繁荣和发展。

桂林旅游学院外国语学院是我国独具特色的外国语学院,旨在培养高素质、国际化旅游外语专业人才。2016年建院以来,院长黄晓萍教授运筹帷幄,锐意进取,大力营造学术气氛,带领团队取得多项可喜成绩。朱江勇教授和同事主编的《西方旅行文学作品选读——以中国形象为视角》正是该院百花园中的一朵奇葩。我衷心祝福该院学科建设日新月异,人才培养硕果累累。

是为序。

陈毅平

暨南大学翻译学院教授、副院长

2017年4月15日

前　言

一、如何理解西方的中国形象

近年来，中国学界在西方的中国形象研究领域取得了一系列突出的成果，随着研究的深入，西方的中国形象研究不断地扩展到文学、历史学、政治学等多个学科，覆盖到跨文化、形象学等多个领域。

西方的中国形象其实是西方人关于中国知识与想象的结果，最早可以追溯到古典时代，从他们对中国虚无缥缈的描述开始，经历了神话般的"丝人国"形象，到文艺复兴时代的"大中华帝国"，随后逐渐变得清晰、具体。以启蒙运动为界，之前西方分三个时期建构出三种不同的"乌托邦"化中国形象：1250—1450 年"大汗的大陆"、1450—1650 年"大中华帝国"、1650—1750 年"孔夫子的中国"。这三种中国形象的共同点都是正面对中国的肯定，从物质到制度观念，从不同层面不断美化中国。肯定与美化中国的意义在于：把中国作为西方现代性社会期望中的"理想楷模"。启蒙时期是西方现代性的确立时期，之后西方又出现了三种中国形象：中华帝国是自由秩序的"他者"——专制的帝国、中华帝国是进步秩序的"他者"——停滞的帝国、中华帝国是文明秩序的"他者"——野蛮或半野蛮的帝国。这三种中国形象的共同点都是对中国的否定，也是从物质到制度观念，从不同层面丑化中国。否定与丑化中国的意义在于：既为西方现代性自我认同提供想象的基础，又为西方殖民扩张提供有效的意识形态。[①] 可见，西方的中国形象是一个动态的历史过程，简单地讲，它是随着西方对中国的观念与认识变化而变化的。

总体上讲，西方的中国形象研究属于一种跨学科的深度观念史研究，它是建立在"异域形象作为文化他者"的理论假设基础上，在西方现代性自我确立与怀疑、自我合法化与自我批判的动态结构中去解析西方现代的中国

① 周宁．世界之中国形象——域外中国形象研究[M]．南京：南京大学出版社，2007.

形象。我们了解、理解、研究西方的中国形象的目的与意义就是认识西方文化中的某一部分，即西方文化中关于中国认识的那一部分。

二、西方旅行文学及研究意义

西方并没有一个明确、具体的地理界限，狭义上的西方仅限于西欧和北美，广义上的西方可能包括整个欧美。文化意义上的西方则是指经济上的资本主义、政治上的民主制度，文化上的启蒙主义——基督教地区。本教材所指的西方是指广义上的西方，即整个欧美以及文化上的基督教地区。另外，与西方相对应的东方也是一个并不明确、具体的地理界限。从文化意义上的东方概念中，中国则是东方最具有代表性的国家，无论是历史的维度还是文化上的维度都最具代表性，中国也是自古以来西方最感兴趣的东方国家之一。

何谓旅行文学？本教材更倾向于当代旅行文学家克利·霍普尔和梯姆·杨斯提出的"吸收了各种不同的风格和文体，不遗余力地转化和融合任何想象中遇到的对手，具有在不同历史时期、不同的学科和不同的视角之间互动潜力"[①]的旅行写作，如航海日志、旅行日记，以及各种类型的游记和旅行故事等构成的丰富庞杂的作品都列为旅行文学。

古今中外大量的旅行文学作品内容的开放性、形式的流动性和风格的多样性，加之旅游学科研究的交叉属性，决定了旅行文学必然会成为人文社科领域关注的焦点之一，旅行文学具有跨文化性和跨学科性，也使其成为比较文学研究的一个重要领域。对旅行文学的考察，我们可以认识到旅行文学笔下的旅游目的地其实是一个超越现世时空的浪漫之地，它既在现实世界中，又不是那个"真实"的地方；旅游目的地的形象不仅是旅行文学文本的产物，而且是旅行者经验的产物，因为旅行者的想象颇具意义；旅游目的地的形象既是一种地理意义上的指向，也是一种文化意义上的指向，不管旅行文学文本的写作环境与现实关系如何，都是以想象或表现的方式构筑一种内心的目的地形象，从这个意义上说，旅行文学的研究对旅游目的地形象研究尤其重要。

---

① ClennHooper，TimYoungs. Perspectives on Travel Writing[M]. London：Ashgate Publishing Limited，2004.

三、西方的中国形象与西方旅行文学

西方的中国形象是在不同时期，用西方文化体系中的既定话语方式，由西方传教士、旅行家、商人、文学家等在历史著作、游记、书信、纯文学作品或哲学著作中关于中国的表述，以历史、哲学、文学作品等诸多文本样式构筑成的关于中国的知识。西方的中国形象反映的不全是中国现实，更多是西方自身关于中国知识的想象与态度，西方旅行文学正是构筑西方的中国形象的大量具体文本中的一种类型。

西方的中国形象的具体文本构筑可以说始于西方旅行文学，即始于蒙元世纪《柏朗嘉宾蒙古纪行》《鲁布鲁克东行记》中关于"契丹"的介绍，随后的《马可波罗游记》《曼德维尔游记》成为当时西方盛赞"人间天堂"的中国形象的典范性文本。在漫长的西方旅行文学发展过程中，大量涉及中国的作品对中国是怎样描绘的？这些作品在不同阶段对中国形象的建构有哪些变化？作品中运用了什么叙述策略、体现了什么意图？这些研究对现实中国作为世界旅游目的地有什么借鉴意义？带着这些问题，本教材选编的西方旅行文学作品包括意大利、英国、法国、美国等广义上西方国家的旅行文学作品。

本教材选择了西方旅行文学中颇具代表性的十四个文本，从西方的中国形象构筑初期为起点，即蒙元世纪的《马可波罗游记》开始，到20世纪30年代的《西行漫记》为止，时间跨度长达七个世纪，从中我们不难看出西方的中国形象所呈现的动态变化。十四个文本基本情况为：《马可波罗游记》和《曼德维尔游记》都盛赞中国的物质文明——丰饶物产与繁华都市；《鲁滨逊漂流记续集》则充斥了对中国人的歧视与偏见，成为西方与中国实力发生变化和西方对中国态度发生变化的信号；《英使谒见乾隆纪实》的背景正值清乾隆盛世，但是西方人看到的是一个沉浸于天朝大国故梦与自给自足状态的中国，这个时段是西方中国形象衰退的重要转折点。晚清时期的作品占大多数，共有八个，包括《中华帝国纪行》《中国五十年见闻录》《我的北京花园》《亲历晚清四十五年》《北京信札》《徒步穿行中国》《扬子江流域及以外地区》和《远东漫游》等。这些作品一方面以西方文化的优越感抨击中国社会的落后与停滞，一方面又对中国传统文化、名胜古迹、民风民俗等方面进行肯定，反映了晚清时期来华旅行者描绘中国时呈现的二重心态。20世纪30年代的《消失的地平线》和《西行漫记》，前者用小说的形式在东方虚构了一

个神秘的、充斥西方观念与价值体系的世外桃源——香格里拉，后者则用新闻纪实的形式对“红色中国”进行全面报道，并准确地预测了中国社会革命运动的未来。

了解、理解、研究西方的中国形象的途径有多种，大量的相关文本阅读是比较直接、有效的一种。限于一本书的篇幅与容量，本教材编选围绕西方的中国形象这一主题，节选十四个文本的某些章节，通过章节的阅读让学生们既对这些文本有初步了解，又可以通过具体文本阅读认识西方的中国形象。我们以西方旅行文学作品为切入点，将中国形象这个话题引入到旅游英语专业本科阶段的课堂教学中，既是一种首创，也是一种尝试，目的在于拓宽学生视野的同时，激发他们对此类问题的关注与探讨的欲望，如果能够达到以上目的，本教材的价值就实现了。

朱江勇

2018年1月22日

于桂林旅游学院

目　录

第一章

马可·波罗游记

一、作品导读

马可·波罗(Marco Polo,1254—1324),13世纪意大利的旅行家、商人,他与鄂多立克、伊本·拔图塔、尼哥罗·康梯一同被誉为"中世纪四大旅行家"。

17岁时,马可·波罗跟随父亲和叔叔,沿陆上丝绸之路前往东方,经两河流域、伊朗高原、帕米尔高原,历时四年的长途旅行,于1275年到达元大都(今北京)。他在中国游历了许多地方,除元大都、行在(杭州)外,还到过云南和东南沿海等地区,并曾担任过元朝官员。1289年,波斯国王阿鲁浑的元妃去世,阿鲁浑派出三位专使到元朝求婚。忽必烈选定阔阔真公主远嫁阿鲁浑,马可·波罗向忽必烈大汗请求参与护送阔阔真公主,完成使命后马可·波罗一家顺路回到意大利。

回国后,马可·波罗在威尼斯和热那亚之间的一次海战中被俘,在狱中他口述了在中国旅行的经历,由其狱友鲁斯蒂谦写下著名的《马可·波罗游记》。

《马可·波罗游记》主要记述马可·波罗在中国的旅行经历,以及途径西亚、中亚和东南亚等一些国家和地区的情况。书中关于中国各地的见闻包括元初的政事、战争、风俗等,以浓重的笔墨记述了元大都的经济、文化、民情风俗,以及西安、开封、南京、扬州、苏州、杭州、福州、泉州等城市和商埠的繁荣景象。

《马可·波罗游记》第一次较全面地向欧洲人介绍了当时东方最富有的国家——中国的物质与精神文明,将中国描绘为财富与权力的世俗天堂,把地大物博、城市繁荣、商业发达、交通便利、君权强盛、政治安定的中国形象展示在世人面前，激起了欧洲人对东方尤其是中国的热烈向往，对以后新航路的开辟产生了巨大的影响。

以下节选的是《马可·波罗游记》中对汗八里（北京）、行在（杭州）的描述，马可·波罗赞叹汗八里（北京）皇宫富丽、行在（杭州）市井繁荣。

二、作品选读

Episode Ⅰ

In the first place is a square enclosed with a wall and deep ditch; each side of the square being eight miles in length, and having at an equal distance from each extremity an entrance-gate, for the concourse of people resorting thither from all quarters. Within this enclosure there is, on the four sides, an open space one mile in breadth, where the troops are stationed. This is bounded by a second wall, enclosing a square of six miles, having three gates on the south side, and three on the north, the middle portal of each being larger than the other two, and always kept shut, excepting on the occasions of the emperor's entrance or departure. Those on each side always remain open for the use of common passengers.

In the middle of each division of these walls is a handsome and spacious building, and consequently within the enclosure there are eight such buildings, in which are deposited the royal military stores; one building being appropriated to the reception of each class of stores. Thus, for instance, the bridles, saddles, stirrups, and other furniture serving for the equipment of cavalry, occupy one storehouse; the bows, strings, quivers, arrows, and other articles belonging to archery, occupy another; cuirasses, corselets, and other armour formed of leather, a third storehouse; and so of the rest.

Within this walled enclosure there is still another, of great thickness, and its height is full twenty-five feet. The battlements or notched parapets are all white. This also forms a square four miles in extent, each side being one mile, and it has six gates, disposed like those of the former enclosure. It contains in like manner eight large buildings, similarly arranged, which are appropriated to the wardrobe of the emperor. The spaces between the one wall and the other are ornamented with many handsome trees, and contain meadows in which are kept various kinds of beasts, such as stags, the animals that yield the musk, roe-bucks, fallow-deer, and others of the same class. Every interval between the walls, not occupied by buildings, is stocked in this manner. The pastures have abundant herbage. The roads across them being raised three feet above their level, and paved, no mud collects upon them, nor rainwater settles, but on the contrary runs off, and contributes to improve the vegetation.

Within these walls, which constitute the boundary of four miles, stands the palace of the Great Khan, the most extensive that has ever yet been known. It reaches from the northern to the southern wall, leaving only a vacant court, where persons of rank and the military guards pass and repass. It has no upper floor, but the roof is very lofty. The paved foundation or platform on which it stands is raised ten spans above the level of the ground, and a wall of marble, two paces wide, is built on all sides. This wall serves as a terrace, where those who walk on it are visible from without. Along the exterior edge of the wall is a handsome balustrade, with pillars, which the people are allowed to approach. The sides of the great halls and the apartments are ornamented with dragons in carved work and gilt, figures of warriors, of birds, and of beasts, with representations of battles. The inside of the roof is contrived in such a manner that nothing besides gilding and painting presents itself to the eye.

On each of the four sides of the palace there is a grand flight of marble steps, by which you ascend from the level of the ground to the wall of marble which surrounds the building, and which constitute the approach to the palace itself.

The grand hall is extremely long and wide, and admits of dinners being there served to great multitudes of people. The palace contains a number of separate chambers, all highly beautiful, and so admirably disposed that it seems impossible to suggest any improvement to the system of their arrangement. The exterior of the roof is adorned with a variety of colors, red, green, azure, and violet, and the sort of covering is so strong as to last for many years. The glazing of the windows is so well wrought and so delicate as to have the transparency of crystal.

In the rear of the body of the palace there are large buildings containing several apartments, where is deposited the private property of the monarch, or his treasure in gold and silver bullion, precious stones, and pearls, and also his vessels of gold and silver plate. Here are likewise the apartments of his wives and concubines; and in this retired situation he dispatches business with convenience, being free from every kind of interruption.

On the other side of the grand palace, and opposite to that in which the emperor resides, is another palace, in every respect similar, appropriated to the residence of Chinghis, his eldest son, at whose court are observed all the ceremonials belonging to that of his father, as the prince who is to succeed to the government of the empire. Not far from the palace, on the northern side, and about a bow-shot distance from the surrounding wall, is an artificial mount of earth, the height of which is full a hundred paces, and the circuit at the base about a mile. It is covered with the most beautiful evergreen trees; for whenever his Majesty receives information of a handsome tree growing in any place, he causes it to be dug up, with all its roots and the earth about them, and however large and heavy it may be, he has it transported by means of elephants to this mount, and adds it to the verdant collection. Because the trees on this hill are always green, it has acquired the name of the Green Mount.

On its summit is erected an ornamental pavilion, which is likewise entirely green. The view of this altogether, — the mount itself, the trees, and the building, form a delightful and at the same time a wonderful scene. In the northern quarter also, and equally within the precincts of the city, there is a large and deep excavation, judiciously formed, the earth from which supplied the material for raising the mount. It is furnished with water by a small rivulet, and has the appearance of a fish-pond, but its use is for watering the cattle.

The stream passing from thence along an aqueduct, at the foot of the Green Mount, proceeds to fill another great and very deep excavation formed between the private palace of the emperor and that of his son Chinghis and the earth from hence equally served to increase the elevation of the mount.

In this latter basin there is great store and variety of fish, from which the table of his Majesty is supplied with any quantity that may be wanted.

The stream discharges itself at the opposite extremity of the piece of water, and precautions are taken to prevent the escape of the fish by placing gratings of copper or iron at the places of its entrance and exit. It is stocked also with swans and other water birds. From the one palace to the other there is a communication by means of a bridge thrown across the water. Such is the description of this great palace.

——**Excerpted from *The Travels of Marco Polo*. 1926: Ch. 10. New York/London: W. W. Norton & Company.**

New Words and Expressions

archery[ˈɑːtʃəri]n. 箭术; 箭法;射箭

armour [ˈɑːmə(r)]n. 装甲;装甲部队;甲胄，盔甲;装甲车辆

ascend [əˈsend]vt. 攀登;继承;占领 vi. 上升;爬坡;追溯

adorn [əˈdɔːn]vt. 佩戴;装饰，修饰;使生色

azure [ˈæʒə(r)]adj. & n. 蔚蓝(的)，天蓝色(的)

bridle [ˈbraidl]n. 缰绳;约束;系带; [航]系船索(链)vt. 抑制，约束;给……套笼头;仰头，昂首 vi. 昂首表示轻蔑;动怒，生气

balustrade [ˌbæləˈstreid]n. (阳台的)栏杆，扶手

bullion [ˈbʊliən]n. 金条;(视为原材料的)金; 银; 金(或银)丝饰带

concourse [ˈkɒŋkɔːs]n. 广场;宽敞的大厅;聚集;群众

corselet [ˈkɔːslit]n. 盔甲，胸衣；前胸

contrive [kənˈtraiv]vt. &vi. 策划；设计，发明；创造；设法做到

concubine [ˈkɒŋkjubain]n. 妾，妃子；情妇

excavation [ˌekskəˈveiʃn]n. 挖掘；开凿；开凿的洞穴（或山路等）；（发掘出来的）古迹

elevation [ˌeliˈveiʃn]n. 高处，高地，高度，海拔；（枪炮的）仰角，射角；升级，上进，向上；高尚；[建]正视图，立视图

gilt [gilt]n. 小母猪；镀金材料；炫目的外表 adj. 镀金的；涂金的 v. 把……镀金

herbage [ˈhɜːbidʒ]n. 牧草；草本，草，草的柔软部分

judiciously [dʒuˈdiʃəsli]adv. 明断地，明智而审慎地

lofty [ˈlɒfti]adj. 高尚的；高耸的，巍峨的；傲慢的

multitude [ˈmʌltitjuːd]n. 大量，许多；大众，人群

ornament [ˈɔːnəmənt]n. 装饰；装饰物；[乐]装饰音 v. 装饰；美化

portal [ˈpɔːtl]n. 入口；桥门；[解剖学]肝门；出孔 adj. [解剖学]门的；肝门的；门静脉的；关于门静脉的

parapet [ˈpærəpit]n. 护墙，矮墙；＜军＞（战壕前作掩护用的）胸墙

precincts [pˈriːsiŋkts]n. 周围地区，四周空地；区域（precinct 的名词复数）；分区；界限；城镇中有某种用途或受限制的地区

quiver [ˈkwivə(r)]vt. & vi. 微颤，抖动 vt. 使震动 n. 抖动；箭筒；颤音

rivulet [ˈrivjələt]n. 小河，小溪

stirrup [ˈstirəp]n. 马镫

stag [stæg]n. 成年牡鹿；阉过的雄畜[牛，猪]；[商]非会员股票经纪人；非真心投资，遇有利机会即行出售股票的认股者 vi. 不带女伴参加晚会；[商]〈俚〉买进新股（等）见利即抛 adj. 全是男人（集会等）的；无异性伴侣的

thither [ˈðiðə(r)]adv. 到那边，向那方 adj. 在那边的，对岸的，那边的

verdant [ˈvɜːdnt]adj. 嫩绿的；（草、田地等）翠绿的；长满绿色植物的；无经验的

wrought [rɔːt]adj. 制造的；加工的；经装饰的；（金属）锤打成形的 vt. 使发生了，造成了（尤指变化）

Notes

1. In the first place is a square enclosed with a wall and deep ditch (Paragraph 1):分词短语作后置定语，相当于一个定语从句。这里 enclosed with... = that(which) is enclosed with...

如:(1) The book written by Luxun sells well. = The book which is written by Luxun sells well.

鲁迅写的那本书很畅销。

(2) The boy standing at the gate is called Peter. = The boy who is standing at the gate is called Peter.

站在门口的男孩叫彼得。

2. In the middle of each division of these walls is a handsome and spacious building(Paragraph 2):在叙述和描写性的句子中，有时为了加强语气或因为主语较长，可把表示地点的介词短语放在句首。如果句子的主要动词是不及物动词，要改变句子的词序，把动词移到主语的前面。

如:(1) Beyond the bushes lay the fields.

树丛的那一边是田野。

(2) Next to it stood a pile of paper cups.

它的旁边放着一摞纸杯。

注意:如果句子的动词是系动词或及物动词，则不可倒装。

如:(1) In the garden everything is peaceful.

花园里一切都是静悄悄的。

(2) Through the windows he could see his kids playing football in the garden.

透过窗户，他看见孩子们在花园里踢足球。

3. Within these walls, which constitute the boundary of four miles, stands the palace of the Great Khan(Paragraph 3):这里的 which constitute the boundary of four miles... 是一个非限制性定语从句。非限制性定语从句主要用于书面语，不用来对所描述的名词加以确定，而是对主句附加说明。

如:(1) My wife, who is out at the moment, will phone you when she gets back.

我的妻子现在出去了，等她回来给你打电话。

(2)I gave him a large glass of whisky, which he drank immediately.
我给了他一大杯威士忌，他马上喝了。

(3)This happened in 1947, when I was a baby.
那件事发生在 1947 年，当时我还是一个婴儿。

Episode Ⅱ

At the end of three days, you reach the noble and magnificent city of Kin-sai [= capital; Hang-chau], a name that signifies "The Celestial City", and which it merits from its pre-eminence to all others in the world, in point of grandeur and beauty, as well as from its abundant delights, which might lead an inhabitant to imagine himself in paradise.

According to common estimation, this city is an hundred miles in circuit. Its streets and canals are extensive, and there are squares, or market-places, which being necessarily proportioned in size to the prodigious concourse of people by whom they are frequented, are exceedingly spacious. It is situated between a lake of fresh and very clear water on the one side, and a river of great magnitude on the other, the waters of which, by a number of canals, large and small, are made to run through every quarter of the city, carrying with them all the filth into the lake, and ultimately to the sea. This furnishes a communication by water, in addition to that by land, to all parts of the town. The canals and the streets being of sufficient width to allow of boats on the one, and carriages in the other, to pass easily with articles necessary for the inhabitants.

It is commonly said that the number of bridges, of all sizes, amounts to twelve thousand. Those which are thrown over the principal canals and are connected with the main streets, have arches so high, and built with so much skill, that vessels with their masts can pass under them. At the same time, carts and horses can pass over, so well is the slope from the street graded to the height of the arch. If they were not so numerous, there would be no way of crossing from one place to another.

Beyond the city, and enclosing it on that side, there is a ditch about forty miles in length， very wide， and full of water that comes from the river before mentioned. This was excavated by the ancient kings of the province， in order that when the river should overflow its banks， the superfluous water might be diverted into this channel. This serves at the same time as a measure of defense. The earth dug out from thence was thrown to the inner side， and has the appearance of many hillocks， surrounding the place.

…

On the borders of the lake are many handsome and spacious edifices belonging to men of rank and great magistrates. There are likewise many idol temples， with their monasteries， occupied by a number of monks， who perform the service of the idols. Near the central part are two islands， upon each of which stands a superb building， with an incredible number of apartments and separate pavilions. When the inhabitants of the city have occasion to celebrate wedding， or to give a sumptuous entertainment， they resort to one of these islands， where they find ready for their purpose every article that can be required， such as vessels， napkins， table linen，and the like， which are provided and kept there at the common expense of the citizens， by whom also the buildings were erected. It may happen that at one time there are a hundred parties assembled there， at wedding or other feasts， all of whom， notwithstanding， are accommodated with separate rooms or pavilions， so judiciously arranged that they do not interfere with each other.

In addition to this， there are upon the lake a great number of pleasure vessels or barges， calculated for holding ten， fifteen， to twenty persons， being from fifteen to twenty paces in length， with a wide and flat flooring， and not liable to heel to either side in passing through the water. Such persons as take delight in the amusement， and mean to enjoy it， either in the company of their women or that of their male companions， engage one of these barges， which are always kept in the nicest order， with proper seats and tables， together with every other kind of furniture necessary for giving an entertainment …

——**Excerpted from *The Travels of Marco Polo*. 1926： Ch. 76. New York/London： W. W. Norton & Company.**

New Words and Expressions

celestial[sə'lestiəl]adj. 天的，天空的 n. 天人，神仙；（指封建时代的）中国人，天朝之人

edifice['edifis]n. 大建筑物；知识的结构

filth [filθ]n. 污秽；污物；猥亵；淫猥

grandeur ['grændʒə(r)]n. 伟大；富丽堂皇；宏伟，壮观

prodigious [prə'didʒəs]adj. 异常的，惊人的；巨大的，庞大的；奇异的；非常的

sumptuous ['sʌmptʃuəs]adj. 豪华的；奢侈的；美轮美奂

superfluous [su:'pɜ:fluəs]adj. 多余的；过多的；不必要的；奢侈的

Notes

1. ...by whom they are frequented, are exceedingly spacious. 在正式用法中，关系代词可用作介词的宾语，介词可置于关系代词之前。指人时，关系代词用 whom；指物时，关系代词用 which。

如：(1)The person to whom I waved just now is our headmaster.

我刚才打招呼的那个人是校长。

(2)They tried to think of a method by which they could save time and money.

他们试图想出一个省钱、省时间的办法。

注意：关系从句中的介词若与动词一起构成短语动词，成为其不可分割的一部分时，介词必须置于动词之后，不可前移到关系代词之前。

如：(1)Everybody I came across seemed to know about it.

我遇见的每个人似乎都知道这件事。

(2)That was the kind of life she was looking forward to.

那就是她向往的那种生活。

2. It is commonly said that... 一些转述所说、所想和所发现的动词常带宾语从句。为避免提及是谁说的话或是谁的想法，常常用非人称代词 it 作先行主语，后接转述动词的被动式。部分可以这样用的动词有：assume,

believe, claim, consider, estimate, expect, find, hope, know, observe, prove, realize, report, say, suppose, think, understand 等。还有一些表示建议、要求、命令等的动词: arrange, demand, desire, insist, order, propose, recommend, require, suggest 等。

如:(1)It is assumed that the government will remain in power.

人们认为本届政府将继续执政。

(2)It is estimated that the work would take two days.

估计这项工作需要两天。

(3)It is suggested that the meeting (should) be put off.

有人建议延期这个会议。

三、思考题

1. 阅读《马可·波罗游记》第二卷中描述元世祖忽必烈和元大都汗八里(北京)的相关章节,了解汗八里在元朝的地理位置及所处的政治、军事、文化、经济地位。

2. 通过对汗八里华丽宫殿的描写,马可·波罗描述的蒙元世纪的中国形象是怎样的?

3. 根据马可·波罗笔下的十三世纪中国杭州的景象,如何理解"明皇朝让中国倒退了整整三百年"?

第二章

曼德维尔游记

一、作品导读

约翰·曼德维尔(John Mandeville),英国中世纪晚期作家,以《曼德维尔游记》闻名于世。

欧洲中世纪晚期关于东方的游记有三部颇具影响:《马可·波罗游记》《鄂多立克东游录》《曼德维尔游记》。其中《马可·波罗游记》后世最著名,在中国生活了17年之久的马可·波罗对中国印象最深的是中国的物质文明;《鄂多立克东游录》最写实,作者鄂多立克是一位传教士,他在"辛迦兰"(广州)登陆,还到刺桐(泉州),他游历中国时既关注中国的财富(世俗关怀),也关注中国的传教(宗教关怀);《曼德维尔游记》则继承了欧洲早期"神游旅行者"写游记的传统,曼德维尔是一位"座椅上的旅行家",他综合了那个时代所有关于东方的传说与事实,用丰富的想象力将他的旅行"见闻"以游记的形式组织起来,写成虚构的散文体游记——《曼德维尔游记》。从当时在欧洲的流传与影响来看,《曼德维尔游记》在三部游记中名列榜首,1500年之前欧洲几乎所有的语种都有《曼德维尔游记》的译本,保存至今的《曼德维尔游记》的手抄本有300种之多,《马可·波罗游记》为143种,《鄂多立克东游录》为70余种。

《曼德维尔游记》中那位虚拟的"旅行者",很可能是一位朝圣者或者十字军骑士,他从英国出发,跨过地中海往东旅行,到东方的第一站就是圣城耶路撒冷,经过了中亚、印度、中国,最后来到传说中的祭司王约翰的国土,并从位于约翰国东海外的伊甸园回到欧洲。《曼德维尔游记》文采斐然,书中的旅行见闻与知识都具有故事性,无论写山川、河流、城郭还是风土人情,都比其他游记要生动有趣。

《曼德维尔游记》同那个时代西方关于东方的游记一样，是以程式化的套话盛赞中国丰饶的物产和繁华的城市，尤其对中国大汗的骑士传奇感兴趣，因而大汉的故事在书中关于中国的章节里占了十分之七的篇幅。正如有学者指出曼德维尔对中国部分的描述是"以骑士传奇的笔法进行杜撰，在当时西方大众文化视野内修正、重塑中国形象。他无意再现中国的现实，而按照当时西方一般想象来描述中国，实际上是西方文化中无意识的欲望。"

二、作品选读

Episode Ⅰ

CATHAY is a great country and a fair, noble and rich, and full of merchants. Thither go merchants all years for to seek spices and all manner of merchandises, more commonly than in any other part. And ye shall understand, that merchants that come from Genoa or from Venice or from Romania or other parts of Lombardy, they go by sea and by land eleven months or twelve, or more sometime, ere they may come to the isle of Cathay that is the principal region of all parts beyond; and it is of the great Chan.

From Cathay go men toward the east by many journeys. And then men find a good city between these others, that men clept Sugarmago. That city is one of the best stored of silk and other merchandises that is in the world.

After go men yet to another old city toward the east. And it is in the province of Cathay. And beside that city the men of Tartary have let make another city that is clept Caydon. And it hath twelve gates, and between the two gates there is always a great mile; so that the two cities, that is to say, the old and the new, have in circuit more than twenty mile.

In this city is the siege of the great Chan in a full great palace and the most passing fair in all the world, of the which the walls be in circuit more than two miles. And within the walls it is all full of other palaces. And in the garden of the great palace there is a great hill, upon which there is another palace; and it is the most fair and the most rich that any man may devise. And all about the palace and the hill be many trees bearing many diverse fruits. And all about that hill be ditches great and deep, and beside them be great vivaria on that one part and on that other. And these is a full fair bridge to pass over the ditches. And in these vivaria be so many wild geese and ganders and wild ducks and swans and herons that it is without number. And all about these ditches and vivaria is the great garden full of wild beasts. So that when the great Chan will have any disport on that, to take any of the wild beasts or of the fowls, he will let chase them and take them at the windows without going out of his chamber.

This palace, where his siege is, is both great and passing fair. And within the palace, in the hall, there be twenty-four pillars of fine gold. And all the wall be covered within of red skins of beasts that men clepe panthers, that be fair beasts and well smelling; so that for the sweet odor of those skins no evil air may enter into the palace. Those skins be as red as blood, and they shine so bright against the sun, that unnethe no man may behold them. And many folk worship those beasts, when they meet them first at morning, for their great virtue and for the good smell that they have, and those skins they prize more than though they were plate of fine gold.

And in the midst of this palace is the montour for great Chan, that is all wrought of gold and of precious stones and great pearls. And at four corners of the mountour be four serpents of gold. And all about there is y-made large nets of silk and gold and great pearls hanging all about the mountour, and under the mountour be conduits of beverage that they drink in the emperor's court. And beside the conduits be many vessels of gold, by which they that be of household drink at the conduit.

And the hall of the palace is full nobly arrayed, and full marvellously attired on all parts in all things that men apparel with any hall. And first, at the chief of the hall is the emperor's throne, full high, where he sitteth at the meat. And that is of fine precious stones, bordered all about with pured gold and precious stones, and great pearls. And the grees that he goeth up to the table be of precious stones mingled with gold.

And at the left side of the emperor's siege is siege of his first wife, one degree lower than the emperor; and it is of jasper, bordered with gold and precious stones. And the siege of his second wife is also another siege, more lower than his first wife; and it is also of jasper, bordered with gold, as that other is. And the siege of the third wife is also more low, by a degree, than the second wife. For he hath always three wives with him, where that ever he be.

——**Excerpted from *The Travels of Sir John Mandeville*. 1905: 139 - 141. London: Macmillan & Co. Limited.**

New Words and Expressions

Cathay [ˈkæθei]n. 中国

Chan [tʃæn]n. 可汗,现在的写法是 khan

thither [ˈðiðə]adv. 向那方;到那边 adj. 对岸的;那边的

merchandise [ˈmɜːtʃəndais]n. 商品;货物 vt. 买卖;推销 vi. 经商

circuit [ˈsɜːkit] 电路,回路;巡回;环道

ditch [ditʃ]vt & vi. 开沟;掘沟 n. 沟渠;壕沟

vivaria [Vaiˈvɜəriə]n. 动物园,植物园

gander [ˈgændə]n. 雄鹅;呆子;一瞥

disport [diˈspɔːt]vt. 使欢娱;使快乐 vi. 娱乐;玩耍 n. 娱乐

panther [ˈpænθə]n. 豹;黑豹;美洲豹

wrought [rɔːt]adj. 锻造的;加工的;精细的

attire [əˈtaiə]n. 服装;盛装 vt. 打扮;使穿衣

apparel [əˈpærəl]n. 服装;衣服 vt. 给……穿衣

pur [pɜː]vi. 发出喉音;咕噜咕噜叫

Notes

By the which they that be of household drink at the conduit (Paragraph 1):by the which 是"介词+关系代词"引导的定语从句，意思是通过某种方式……，现代英语 which 前面的"the"省略。

如:(1)The bike by which I went to school was stolen.

我上学骑的自行车丢了。

(2)The book by which I acquire much knowledge of adventure is now a very best-selling one.

我学到了不少冒险知识的那本书现在很畅销。

Episode Ⅱ

First I shall say why he was clept the great Chan. Ye shall understand, that all the world was destroyed by Noah's flood, save only Noah and his wife and his children. Noah had three sons, Shem, Cham, and Japhet. This Cham was he that saw his father's privy members naked when he slept, and scorned them, and shewed them with his finger to his brethren in scorning wise. And therefore he was cursed of God. And Japhet turned his face away and covered them.

These three brethren had seisin in all the land. And this Cham, for his cruelty, took the greater and the best part, toward the east, that is clept Asia, and Shem took Africa, and Japhet took Europe. And therefore is all the earth parted in these three parts by these three brethren. Cham was the greatest and the most mighty, and of him came more generation than of the other. And of his son Chuse was engendered Nimrod the giant, that was the first King of that ever was in the world, and he began the foundation of the tower of Babylon. And that time, the fiends of hell came many times and lay with the women of his generation and engendered on them diverse folk, as monsters and folk disfigured, some without heads, some with great ears, some with one eye, some giants, some with horses' feet, and many other diverse shape against kind. And of that generation of Cham become the Paynims and divers folk that be in isles of the sea by all Ind. And forasmuch as he was the most mighty, and no man might withstand him, he cleped himself the Son of God and sovereign of all the world. And for this Cham, this emperor clepeth him Cham, and sovereign of all the world.

——**Excerpted from *The Travels of Sir John Mandeville*. 1905: 145. London: Macmillan & Co. Limited.**

New Words and Expressions

brethren [ˈbrəðrən]n. 弟兄们;同胞

seisin [ˈsizin]n. 依法占有(财)产

privy [ˈprivi]adj. 私人的;不公开的;秘密参与的 n. 有利害关系的人

scorn [skɔːn]n. 轻蔑;嘲笑;藐视的对象 vt. & vi. 轻蔑;藐视

cham [kæm]n. 可汗

disfigure [disˈfigə]vt. 使变丑;损毁……的外形;使大为减色

mighty [ˈmaiti]adj. 有力的;强有力的;有势力的 n. 有势力的人

sovereign [ˈsɒvrin]adj. 至高无上的;有主权的 n. 君主;独立国

Notes

And forasmuch as he was the most mighty, and no man might withstand him (paragraph 2):这里 forasmuch 作连词,表示"鉴于……,所以"。

如:Forasmuch as the sins he committed, he is sentenced to death.

鉴于他的罪行,他被处死刑。

Episode Ⅲ

Now shall I tell you the governance of the court of the great Chan, when he marketh solemn feasts; and that is principally four times in the year.

The first feast of his birth, that other is of his presentation in their temple that they clepe their Moseache, where they make a manner of circumcision, and the tother two feasts be of his idols. The first feast of the idols is when he is first put into their temple and throned. The tother feast when the idol beginneth first to speak, or to work miracles. More be there not of solemn feasts, but if he marry any of his children.

Now understand, that at every of these feasts he hath great multitude of people, well ordained and well arrayed, by thousands, by hundreds, and by tens. And every man knoweth well what service he shall do, and every man giveth so good heed and so good attendance to his service that no man findeth no default. And there be first ordained 4000 barons, mighty and rich, for to govern and to make ordinance for the feast, and for to serve the emperor. And these solemn feasts be made without in halls and tents made of cloths of gold and of tartaries, full nobly. And all those barons have crowns of gold upon their heads, full noble and rich, full of precious stones and great pearls orient. And they be all clothed in cloths of gold or of tartaries or of camakas, so richly and so perfectly, that no man in the world can amend it, ne better devise it. And all those robes be orfrayed all about, and dubbed full of precious stones and of great orient pearls, full richly. And they may well do so, for cloths of gold and of silk be greater cheap there a great deal than be cloths of wool. And these 4000 barons be devised in four companies, and every thousand is clothed in cloths all of one color, and that so well arrayed and so richly, that it is marvel to behold.

The first thousand, that is of dukes, of earls, of marquises and of admirals, all clothed in cloths of gold, with tissues of green silk, and bordered with gold full of precious stones in manner as I have said before. The second thousand is all clothed in cloths diapered of red silk, all wrought with gold, and the orfrays set full of great pearl and precious stones, full nobly wrought. The third thousand is clothed in cloths of silk, of purple or of Ind. And the fourth thousand is in cloths of yellow. And all their clothes be so nobly and so richly wrought with gold and precious stones and rich pearls, that if a man of this country had but only one of their robes, he might well say that he should never be poor; for the gold and the precious stones and the great orient pearls be of greater value on this half the sea than they be beyond the sea in those countries.

——Excerpted from *The Travels of Sir John Mandeville*. 1905: 151 - 153. London: Macmillan & Co. Limited.

New Words and Expressions

governance [ˈgʌv(ə)nəns]n. 管理;统治;支配
principally [ˈprinsəpli]adv. 主要地;大部分
circumcision [sɜːkəmˈsiʒ(ə)n]n. 割礼;净心
tother [tʌðə]pron. 另一个,是 the other 的古英语说法
throne [θrəun]n. 登基,登上王位
multitude [ˈmʌltitud]n. 群众;多数
ordain [ɔːˈdein]vt. 任命某人为牧师;授某人以圣职 vi. 颁布命令
knotweed [ˈnɒtˌwiːd]n. 紫菀科植物; 蓼科杂草; 节草
giveth [givð]v. gives 的古英语写法
baron [ˈbærən]n. 男爵;大亨;巨头
ternary [ˈtɜːnəri]adj. 三元的; 三进制的;第三的
dub [dʌb]vt. 配音;轻点;授予称号 n. 笨蛋;鼓声
duke [djuːk]n. 公爵; (公国的)君主
earl [ɜːl]n. (英)伯爵
marquis [ˈmɑːkwis]n. (法)侯爵;世袭贵族
diaper [ˈdɑiəpə]n. 尿布 vt. 给孩子换尿布
Ind [ind]abbr. 印第安纳州;印度
robe [rəʊb]n. 长袍; 礼服 vi. 穿长袍 vt. 使穿长袍

Notes

he might well say that he should never be poor (paragraph 4):这里 may [might] well 主要用于加强推测的语气,表示具有较大的可能性。

如：(1) He might well lose his job.

他多半会丢了那份工作。

(2) He might well find that the course is too difficult.

他很可能觉得这门课太难。

三、思考题

1. 曼德维尔是一位在座椅上“神游”的旅行家，他用丰富的想象力将他的旅行“见闻”以游记的形式组织起来。他笔下的中国形象是怎样的？

2.《曼德维尔游记》文笔生动有趣、文采斐然，书中哪些方面体现了这些特点？

第三章

鲁滨逊漂流记续集

一、作品导读

丹尼尔·笛福(Daniel Defoe,1660—1731 年),出生于英国伦敦,他是英国启蒙时期现实主义小说的奠基人,享有欧洲的“小说之父”“英国小说之父”“英国报纸之父”等美誉。1719 年,他发表第一部小说《鲁滨逊漂流记》获得巨大成功,小说成功地塑造了一个乐观、勇敢,靠智慧与勇气战胜困难的理想化资产者——鲁滨逊,这部小说大受读者欢迎,鲁滨逊形象也成为当时社会追求冒险、倡导个人奋斗风气的代言人。丹尼尔·笛福的代表性作品除《鲁滨逊漂流记》之外,还有《摩尔·弗兰德斯》《杰克上校》《鲁滨逊漂流记续集》等。

《鲁滨逊漂流记续集》写作的时期,是西方中国形象出现大转折的时期,此时西方人追慕、美化中国的时代逐渐过去,开始进入丑化憎恶中国的阶段。西方的中国形象塑造的历史起点是在 1250 年前后,即蒙元时代《柏朗嘉宾蒙古纪行》《鲁布鲁克东行记》对“契丹”的描述,随后的《马可波罗游记》和《曼德维尔游记》成为当时盛赞“人间天堂”的中国形象的经典性著作。《鲁滨逊漂流记续集》中的鲁滨逊借着环球旅行来到当时中国两个比较大的城市——南京和北京,以及长城以外的蒙古地区。书中鲁滨逊在南京 10 天旅行的所见所闻,让鲁滨逊觉得尽管南京人口繁盛,但是同英国相比仍然是毫无可称道之处——不管是中国人的衣着、生活方式,还是政府、宗教以及财产与荣耀等方面都不值得一提。书中还借鲁滨逊在北京旅行期间的所见,将随从的总督塑造成贪婪、傲慢的形象,其他中国人无论富人穷人,不是喜欢摆架子就是很傲慢无礼,充满了对中国人的歧视与偏见。

丹尼尔·笛福本身并没有到过东方，书中鲁滨逊在中国游历是以他的殖民主义者的眼光和欧洲中心主义优越感的心态编纂加工创作而成，实际上是作者借鲁滨逊在中国的旅行表达经历资产阶级革命逐渐强大的英国，对沉浸在落日余晖中的中国的贬斥和轻视。《鲁滨逊漂流记续集》对中国的态度，既是东西方实力关系开始发生变化的信号——英国迅速崛起而中国社会发展依然缓慢，也是西方人开始从精神和物质上寻求对中国进行殖民扩张与统治的理论依据——要将中国这个文明古国变成殖民地，首先要诋毁它，然后用大炮来摧毁它。也就是说，《鲁滨逊漂流记续集》对中国的排斥是欧洲殖民主义的序曲，它为欧洲殖民扩展舆论宣传的文本基础，对当今我们研究跨文化交流有着一定的警醒作用。

二、作品选读

Episode Ⅰ

First, we went ten days' journey to Nankin, a city well worth seeing; they say it has a million of people in it: it is regularly built, and the streets are all straight, and cross one another in direct lines. But when I come to compare the miserable people of these countries with ours, their fabrics, their manner of living, their government, their religion, their wealth, and their glory, as some call it, I must confess that I scarcely think it worth my while to mention them here. We wonder at the grandeur, the riches, the pomp, the ceremonies, the government, the manufactures, the commerce, and conduct of these people; not that there is really any matter for wonder, but because, having a true notion of the barbarity of those countries, the rudeness and the ignorance that prevail there, we do not expect to find any such thing so far off. Otherwise, what are their buildings to the palaces and royal buildings of Europe? What their trade to the universal commerce of England, Holland, France, and Spain? What are their cities to ours, for wealth, strength, gaiety of apparel, rich furniture, and infinite variety? What are their ports, supplied with a few junks and barks, to our navigation, our merchant fleets, our large and powerful navies? Our city of London has more trade than half their mighty empire: one English, Dutch, or French man-of-war of eighty guns would be able to fight almost all the shipping belonging to China: but the greatness of their wealth, their trade, the power of their government, and the strength of their armies, may be a little surprising to us, because, as I have said, considering them as a barbarous nation of pagans, little better than savages, we did not expect such things among them. But all the forces of their empire, though they were to bring two millions of men into the field together, would be able to do nothing but ruin the country and starve themselves; a million of their foot could not stand before one embattled body of our infantry, posted so as not to be surrounded, though they were not to be one to twenty in number; nay, I do not boast if I say that thirty thousand German or English foot, and ten thousand horse, well managed, could defeat all the forces of China. Nor is there a fortified town in China that could hold out one month against the batteries and attacks of an European army. They have firearms, it is true, but they are awkward and uncertain in their going off; and their powder has but little strength. Their armies are badly disciplined, and want skill to attack, or temper to retreat; and therefore, I must confess, it seemed strange to me, when I came home, and heard our people say such fine things of the power, glory, magnificence, and trade of the Chinese; because, as far as I saw, they appeared to be a contemptible herd or crowd of ignorant, sordid slaves, subjected to a government qualified only to rule such a people; and were not its distance inconceivably, great from Muscovy, and that empire in a manner as rude, impotent, and ill governed as they, the Czar of Muscovy might with ease drive them all out of their country, and conquer them in one campaign; and had the Czar (who is now a growing prince) fallen this way, instead of attacking the warlike Swedes, and equally improved himself in the art of war, as they say he has done; and if none of the powers of Europe had envied or interrupted him, he might by this time have been Emperor of China, instead of being beaten by the King of Sweden at Narva, when the latter was not one to six in number.

As their strength and their grandeur, so their navigation, commerce, and husbandry are very imperfect, compared to the same things in Europe; also, in their knowledge, their learning, and in their skill in the sciences, they are either very awkward or defective, though they have globes or spheres, and a smattering of the mathematics, and think they know more than all the world besides. But they know little of the motions of the heavenly bodies; and so grossly and absurdly ignorant are their common people, that when the sun is eclipsed, they think a great dragon has assaulted it, and is going to run away with it; and they fall a clattering with all the drums and kettles in the country, to fright the monster away, just as we do to hive a swarm of bees!

As this is the only excursion of the kind which I have made in all the accounts I have given of my travels, so I shall make no more such. It is none of my business, nor any part of my design; but to give an account of my own adventures through a life of inimitable wanderings, and a long variety of changes, which, perhaps, few that come after me will have heard the like of: I shall, therefore, say very little of all the mighty places, desert countries, and numerous people I have yet to pass through, more than relates to my own story, and which my concern among them will make necessary.

I was now, as near as I can compute, in the heart of China, about thirty degrees north of the line, for we were returned from Nankin. I had indeed a mind to see the city of Pekin, which I had heard so much of, and Father Simon importuned me daily to do it. At length his time of going away being set, and the other missionary who was to go with him being arrived from Macao, it was necessary that we should resolve either to go or not; so I referred it to my partner, and left it wholly to his choice, who at length resolved it in the affirmative, and we prepared for our journey. We set out with very good advantage as to finding the way; for we got leave to travel in the retinue of one of their mandarins, a kind of viceroy or principal magistrate in the province where they reside, and who take great state upon them, travelling with great attendance, and great homage from the people, who are sometimes greatly impoverished by them, being obliged to furnish provisions for them and all their attendants in their journeys. I particularly observed in our travelling with his baggage, that though we received sufficient provisions both for ourselves and our horses from the country, as belonging to the mandarin, yet we were obliged to pay for everything we had, after the market price of the country, and the mandarin's steward collected it duly from us. Thus our travelling in the retinue of the mandarin, though it was a great act of kindness, was not such a mighty favour to us, but was a great advantage to him, considering there were above thirty other people travelled in the same manner besides us, under the protection of his retinue; for the country furnished all the provisions for nothing to him, and yet he took our money for them.

——**Excerpted from *The Further Adventures of Robinson Crusoe*. 2000: Ch. 13. Philadelphia: Penn State University Press.**

New Words and Expressions

fabric [ˈfæbrik]n. 纤维织物

confess [kənˈfes]vt. 承认;坦白;忏悔;供认 vi. 承认;坦白;忏悔;供认

grandeur [ˈgræn(d)ʒə]n. 壮丽;庄严;宏伟

pomp [pɒmp]n. 盛况;浮华;壮丽;夸耀

barbarity [bɑːˈbæriti]n. 残暴;粗野

gaiety [ˈgeiəti]n. 快乐,兴高采烈;庆祝活动,喜庆;(服饰)华丽,艳丽

navigation [næviˈgeiʃ(ə)n]n. 航行;航海

fleet [fliːt]adj. 快速的,敏捷的 n. 舰队;港湾;小河 vi. 飞逝;疾驰;掠过 vt. 消磨

barbarous [ˈbɑːb(ə)rəs]adj. 野蛮的;残暴的

pagan [ˈpeig(ə)n]adj. 异教的;异教徒的 n. 异教徒;无宗教信仰者

embattle [imˈbæt(ə)l]vt. 布阵;列阵;整军备战;严阵以待

infantry [ˈinf(ə)ntri]n. 步兵；步兵团

nay [nei]adv. 不；甚至；不仅如此 n. 拒绝；反对；投反对票的人

fortify [ˈfɔːtifai]vt. 加强；增强；(酒)的酒精含量；设防于 vi. 筑防御工事

firearm [ˈfaiəraːm]n. 火器；枪炮

retreat [riˈtriːt]n. 撤退；休息寓所；撤退 vi. 撤退；退避；向后倾 vt. 退(棋)；使后退

contemptible [kənˈtem(p)tib(ə)l]adj. 可鄙的；卑劣的；可轻视的

sordid [ˈsɔːdid]adj. 肮脏的；卑鄙的；利欲熏心的；色彩暗淡的

inconceivably [ˌinkənˈsivəbli]adv. 不可思议地

impotent [ˈimpət(ə)nt]adj. 无力的；无效的；虚弱的；阳痿的

husbandry [ˈhʌzbəndri]n. 饲养；务农，耕种；家政

smattering [ˈsmætəriŋ]n. 一知半解；少数；略知 adj. 肤浅的；些许的；点滴的

assault [əˈsɔːlt]n. 攻击；袭击 vt. 攻击；袭击 vi. 袭击；动武

clatter [ˈklætə]n. 哗啦声；咔嗒声 vi. 发出哗啦声；喧闹的谈笑 vt. 使咔嗒地响

inimitable [iˈnimitəb(ə)l]adj. 独特的；无比的；无法仿效的

compute [kəmˈpjuːt]vt. 计算；估算 vi. 计算；估算；推断 n. 计算；估计；推断

importune [ˌimpɔːˈtjuːn]vi. 强求；胡搅蛮缠 vt. 强求；一再向某人要求

retinue [ˈretinjuː]n. 随行人员；扈从

viceroy [ˈvaisrɒi]n. 总督；(北美)一种黑色蝴蝶

magistrate [ˈmædʒistrət]n. 地方法官；文职官员；治安推事

homage [ˈhɒmidʒ]n. 敬意；尊敬；效忠

impoverish [imˈpɒv(ə)riʃ]vt. 使贫穷；使枯竭

furnish [ˈfɜːniʃ]vt. 提供；供应；装备

steward [ˈstjuːəd]n. 管家；乘务员；膳务员；工会管事 vi. 当服务员；当管事 vt. 管理

Notes

1. as far as I saw, they appeared to be a contemptible herd or crowd of ignorant, sordid slaves, subjected to a government qualified only to rule such a people(paragraph 1):此处的 be subjected to 意为“屈从于，遭受”。

如:(1)Media is not subjected to political pressure.

媒体不受政治压力的束缚。

(2)The city was subjected to heavy bombing.

那座城市遭受到猛烈轰炸。

2. and had the Czar (who is now a growing prince) fallen this way, instead of attacking the warlike Swedes(paragraph 1):这里的 had the Czar fallen... 是 if 引导的虚拟条件状语从句的省略。在虚拟条件句中，有时可将引导虚拟条件句的连词 if 省略，用倒装句型，即将从句中的 had、were、should 等提到句首。

如:(1)If he were here, she would agree too.

Were he here, she would agree too.

(2)If we had found him earlier, we could have saved his life.

Had we found him earlier, we could have saved his life.

(3)If any visitors should come, I would say you are not in.

Should any visitors come, I would say you are not in.

3. who are sometimes greatly impoverished by them, being obliged to furnish provisions for them and all their attendants in their journeys (paragraph 4):此处的 be obliged to 意为“不得不;有义务;感谢;被迫做”等，也可以用 feel obliged to do something。

如:(1) They were obliged to sell their house in order to pay their debts.

他们被迫卖房还债。

(2)I felt obliged to invite him into the parlor.

我只得把他让进客厅。

Episode Ⅱ

We were twenty-five days travelling to Pekin, through a country exceeding populous, but I think badly cultivated; the husbandry, the economy, and the way of living miserable, though they boast so much of the industry of the people: I say miserable, if compared with our own, but not so to these poor wretches, who know no other. The pride of the poor people is infinitely great, and exceeded by nothing but their poverty, in some parts, which adds to that which I call their misery; and I must needs think the savages of America live much more happy than the poorer sort of these, because as they have nothing, so they desire nothing; whereas these are proud and insolent and in the main are in many parts mere beggars and drudges. Their ostentation is inexpressible; and, if they can, they love to keep multitudes of servants or slaves, which is to the last degree ridiculous, as well as their contempt of all the world but themselves.

I must confess I travelled more pleasantly afterwards in the deserts and vast wildernesses of Grand Tartary than here, and yet the roads here are well paved and well kept, and very convenient for travellers; but nothing was more awkward to me than to see such a haughty, imperious, insolent people, in the midst of the grossest simplicity and ignorance; and my friend Father Simon and I used to be very merry upon these occasions, to see their beggarly pride. For example, coming by the house of a country gentleman, as Father Simon called him, about ten leagues off the city of Nanking, we had first of all the honour to ride with the master of the house about two miles; the state he rode in was a perfect Don Quixotism, being a mixture of pomp and poverty. His habit was very proper for a merry-andrew, being a dirty calico, with hanging sleeves, tassels, and cuts and slashes almost on every side: it covered a taffety vest, so greasy as to testify that his honour must be a most exquisite sloven. His horse was a poor, starved, hobbling creature, and two slaves followed him on foot to drive the poor creature along; he had a whip in his hand, and he belaboured the beast as fast about the head as his slaves did about the tail; and thus he rode by us, with about ten or twelve servants, going from the city to his country seat, about half a league before us. We travelled on gently, but this figure of a gentleman rode away before us; and as we stopped at a village about an hour to refresh us, when we came by the country seat of this great man, we saw him in a little place before his door, eating a repast. It was a kind of garden, but he was easy to be seen; and we were given to understand that the more we looked at him the better he would be pleased. He sat under a tree, something like the palmetto, which effectually shaded him over the head, and on the south side; but under the tree was placed a large umbrella, which made that part look well enough. He sat lolling back in a great elbow-chair, being a heavy corpulent man, and had his meat brought him by two women slaves. He had two more, one of whom fed the squire with a spoon, and the other held the dish with one hand, and scraped off what he let fall upon his worship's beard and taffety vest.

Leaving the poor wretch to please himself with our looking at him, as if we admired his idle pomp, we pursued our journey. Father Simon had the curiosity to stay to inform himself what dainties the country justice had to feed on in all his state, which he had the honour to taste of, and which was, I think, a mess of boiled rice, with a great piece of garlic in it, and a little bag filled with green pepper, and another plant which they have there, something like our ginger, but smelling like musk, and tasting like mustard; all this was put together, and a small piece of lean mutton boiled in it, and this was his worship's repast. Four or five servants more attended at a distance, who we supposed were to eat of the same after their master. As for our mandarin with whom we travelled, he was respected as a king, surrounded always with his gentlemen, and attended in all his appearances with such pomp, that I saw little of him but at a distance. I observed that there was not a horse in his retinue but that our carrier's packhorses in England seemed to me to look much better; though it was hard to judge rightly, for they were so covered with equipage, mantles, trappings, &c.,

that we could scarce see anything but their feet and their heads as they went along.

I was now light-hearted, and all my late trouble and perplexity being over, I had no anxious thoughts about me, which made this journey the pleasanter to me; in which no ill accident attended me, only in passing or fording a small river, my horse fell and made me free of the country, as they call it - that is to say, threw me in. The place was not deep, but it wetted me all over. I mention it because it spoiled my pocket-book, wherein I had set down the names of several people and places which I had occasion to remember, and which not taking due care of, the leaves rotted, and the words were never after to be read.

——Excerpted from *The Further Adventures of Robinson Crusoe*. 2000: Ch. 13. Philadelphia: Penn State University Press.

New Words and Expressions

populous [ˈpɒpjʊləs]adj. 人口稠密的;人口多的

wretch [retʃ]n. 可怜的人，不幸的人;卑鄙的人

insolent [ˈins(ə)l(ə)nt]adj. 无礼的;傲慢的;粗野的;无耻的

drudge [drʌdʒ]vi. 做苦工，干苦力 vt. 强迫做苦工 n. 做苦工的人

ostentation [ˌɒstenˈteiʃ(ə)n]n. 卖弄;虚饰;虚有其表

multitude [ˈmʌltitjuːd]n. 群众;多数

haughty [ˈhɔːti]adj. 傲慢的;自大的

imperious [imˈpiəriəs]adj. 专横的;迫切的;傲慢的

merry-andrew 戏班小丑;丑角; 滑稽演员

calico [ˈkælikəʊ]n. (美)印花棉布;(英)白棉布 adj. 印花棉布的;有斑点的

tassel [ˈtæs(ə)l]n. 流苏;缨;穗 vt. 用流苏装饰;摘下……穗 vi. 抽穗;长出穗状雄花

slash [slæʃ]vt. 猛砍;鞭打;严厉批评 vi. 猛砍;严厉批评 n. 削减;斜线;猛砍

taffety [ˈtæfiti]n. 平纹皱丝织品

greasy [ˈgriːsi; —zi]adj. 油腻的；含脂肪多的；谄媚的

testify [ˈtestifai]vt. 证明，证实；作证　vi. 作证；证明

exquisite [ˈekskwizit]adj. 精致的；细腻的；优美的，高雅的；异常的；剧烈的

sloven [ˈslʌv(ə)n]n. 懒散的人；不修边幅的人

hobble [ˈhɒb(ə)l]vi. 蹒跚；跛行　vt. 使跛行　n. 跛行步态

belabour [biˈlebə]vt. 痛打；不断辱骂和嘲弄

repast [riˈpɑːst]n. 就餐，饮食　vi. 就餐；设宴

palmetto [pælˈmetəʊ]n. 美洲蒲葵(棕榈科植物)

loll [lɒl]vi. 懒洋洋地倚靠　vt. 懒洋洋地倚靠

corpulent [ˈkɔːpjʊl(ə)nt]adj. 肥胖的

squire [skwaiə]n. 乡绅；侍从；大地主；地方法官　vt. 随侍；护卫

dainty [ˈdeinti]adj. 美味的；讲究的；秀丽的；挑剔的　n. 美味

ginger [ˈdʒindʒə]n. 姜；姜黄色；精力；有姜味　vt. 用姜给……调味；使某人有活力

musk [mʌsk]n. 麝香；麝香鹿；麝香香味

mustard [ˈmʌstəd]n. 芥末；芥菜；深黄色；强烈的兴趣

packhorse [ˈpækhɔːs]n. 驮马

equipage [ˈekwipidʒ]n. 装备，用具；马车及侍从

mantle [ˈmænt(ə)l]n. 地幔；斗篷；覆盖物 vi. 覆盖；脸红 vt. 覆盖

ford [fɔːd]n. 浅滩 vi. 涉水而过 vt. 涉过；徒涉

Notes

1. though they boast so much of the industry of the people(paragraph 1)：此处的 boast of 意为"自吹自擂，吹嘘，夸耀，自夸或以有……而自豪，自负有，拥有(通常是可以自豪的东西)"等。

如：(1)Everyone in this small city boasts of its beautiful scenery.

这座小城的人都以这座城市的美丽景色而自豪。

(2)He is used to boasting of his great wealth.

他习惯于夸耀他的巨额财富。

2. I was now light-hearted, and all my late trouble and perplexity

being over(paragraph 4)：在书面语中，如果分词短语的主语不同于句子的主语，可以在分词短语前另加一个主语。使用这一结构时，分词的主语与主要动词的主语通常有密切的联系，分词常为 being 或 having。

如：(1)John having run a red light, the police arrested him.

约翰由于闯红灯被警察逮捕了。

(2)That being the case, we'd better make some changes in the plan.

要是情况是那样，我们还是把计划改一改。

Episode Ⅲ

At length we arrived at Pekin. I had nobody with me but the youth whom my nephew had given me to attend me as a servant and who proved very trusty and diligent; and my partner had nobody with him but one servant, who was a kinsman. As for the Portuguese pilot, he being desirous to see the court, we bore his charges for his company, and for our use of him as an interpreter, for he understood the language of the country, and spoke good French and a little English. Indeed, this old man was most useful to us everywhere; for we had not been above a week at Pekin, when he came laughing. "Ah, Seignior Inglese," says he, "I have something to tell will make your heart glad."—"My heart glad," says I; "what can that be? I don't know anything in this country can either give me joy or grief to any great degree."—"Yes, yes," said the old man, in broken English, "make you glad, me sorry."—"Why," said I, "will it make you sorry?"—"Because," said he, "you have brought me here twenty-five days' journey, and will leave me to go back alone; and which way shall I get to my port afterwards, without a ship, without a horse, without Pecune?" so he called money, being his broken Latin, of which he had abundance to make us merry with. In short, he told us there was a great caravan of Muscovite and Polish merchants in the city, preparing to set out on their journey by land to Muscovy, within four or five weeks; and he was sure we would take the opportunity to go with them, and leave him behind, to go back alone.

I confess I was greatly surprised with this good news, and had scarce power to speak to him for some time; but at last I said to him, "How do you know this? are you sure it is true?"—"Yes," says he; "I met this morning in the street an old acquaintance of mine, an Armenian, who is among them. He came last from Astrakhan, and was designed to go to Tonquin, where I formerly knew him, but has altered his mind, and is now resolved to go with the caravan to Moscow, and so down the river Volga to Astrakhan."—"Well, Seignior," says I, "do not be uneasy about being left to go back alone; if this be a method for my return to England, it shall be your fault if you go back to Macao at all." We then went to consult together what was to be done; and I asked my partner what he thought of the pilot's news, and whether it would suit with his affairs? He told me he would do just as I would; for he had settled all his affairs so well at Bengal, and left his effects in such good hands, that as we had made a good voyage, if he could invest it in China silks, wrought and raw, he would be content to go to England, and then make a voyage back to Bengal by the Company's ships.

Having resolved upon this, we agreed that if our Portuguese pilot would go with us, we would bear his charges to Moscow, or to England, if he pleased; nor, indeed, were we to be esteemed over-generous in that either, if we had not rewarded him further, the service he had done us being really worth more than that; for he had not only been a pilot to us at sea, but he had been like a broker for us on shore; and his procuring for us a Japan merchant was some hundreds of pounds in our pockets. So, being willing to gratify him, which was but doing him justice, and very willing also to have him with us besides, for he was a most necessary man on all occasions, we agreed to give him a quantity of coined gold, which, as I computed it, was worth one hundred and seventy-five pounds sterling, between us, and to bear all his charges, both for himself and horse, except only a horse to carry his goods. Having settled this between ourselves, we called him to let him know what we had resolved. I told him he had complained of our being willing to let him go back alone, and I was now about to tell him we designed he should not go back at all. That as we had resolved to go to Europe with the caravan, we were very willing he should go with us; and that we called him to know his mind. He shook his head and said it was a long journey, and that he had no Pecune to carry him thither, or to subsist himself when he came there. We told him we believed it was so, and therefore we had resolved to do something for him that should let him see how sensible we were of the service he had done us, and also how agreeable he was to us: and then I told him what we had resolved to give him here, which he might lay out as we would do our own; and that as for his charges, if he would go with us we would set him safe on shore (life and casualties excepted), either in Muscovy or England, as he would choose, at our own charge, except only the carriage of his goods. He received the proposal like a man transported, and told us he would go with us over all the whole world; and so we all prepared for our journey. However, as it was with us, so it was with the other merchants: they had many things to do, and instead of being ready in five weeks, it was four months and some days before all things were got together.

——**Excerpted from *The Further Adventures of Robinson Crusoe*. 2000: Ch. 13. Philadelphia: Penn State University Press.**

New Words and Expressions

kinsman ['kinzmən]n. 男性亲戚；同族者

desirous [di'zaiərəs]adj. 渴望的；想要的

caravan ['kærəvæn]n. （可供居住的）拖车；大篷车；旅行队（如商队） vi. 乘拖车度假

acquaintance [ə'kweint(ə)ns]n. 熟人；相识；了解；知道

wrought [rɔːt]adj. 锻造的；加工的；精细的 v. 工作（work 的过去分词）

procure [prə'kjʊə]vt. 获得；取得；导致 vi. 取得

gratify ['grætifai]vt. 使满足；使满意；使高兴

sterling ['stɜːliŋ]adj. 纯正的；英币的；纯银制的 n. 英国货币；标准纯银

thither [ˈðiðə]adv. 向那方；到那边　adj. 对岸的；那边的

subsist [səbˈsist]vi. 存在；维持生活　vt. 供养

Notes

1. As for the Portuguese pilot, he being desirous to see the court, we bore his charges for his company(paragraph 1)：这里 he being desirous to see the court 属于是现在分词作原因状语，修饰后面的 we bore his charges for his company。

如：He being ill, I had to stay at home.

他生病了，所以我不得不待在家里。

2. He came last from Astrakhan, and was designed to go to Tonquin, where I formerly knew him(paragraph 3)：这里的 where 用于引导定语从句。这句话中先行词表示具体地点，并且在定语从句中做状语。

如：This is the house where I once lived.

此外，先行词是表示抽象地点的 point, case, position, condition, activity, situation 等，并作状语，也可用 where 引导。

如：(1) You reach a point where medicine can't help.

你已到了药物无法治疗的地步。

(2) She wants a job where her management skills can be put to good use.

她想找一份能将她的管理技能派上用场的工作。

3. Having resolved upon this, we agreed that if our Portuguese pilot would go with us(paragraph 4)；Having settled this between ourselves, we called him to let him know what we had resolved(paragraph 4)：这两个句子中句首都用到了 having done，属于现在分词的完成式，用作状语，表示时间、原因、结果等。

如：(1) Having bought our tickets, we went into the theatre.

我们买好票后就进了剧院。

(2) Having lived in Nanjing for many years, he knows the place very well.

在南京生活了很多年，他对这个地方非常了解。

三、思考题

1. 在作品中，丹尼尔·笛福为什么把中国称为“一个傲慢专横、粗鲁无礼的民族”？

2. 与《马可·波罗游记》相比较，你如何理解丹尼尔·笛福作品中关于中国形象描述的狭隘性和片面性？

第四章

英使谒见乾隆纪实

一、作品导读

乔治·伦纳德·斯当东(Sir George Leonard Staunton,1st Baronet,1737—1801),出生于爱尔兰戈尔韦郡,第一代斯当东从男爵,英国探险家、植物学家,受雇于不列颠东印度公司。斯当东先后获得医学和法学博士学位,1784 年,斯当东与好友乔治·马戛尔尼一起前往马德拉斯,同蒂普苏丹缔结和约。因为这个功绩,斯当东 1785 年获得从男爵的爵位,1787 年入选英国皇家学会院士,代表性著作有《英使谒见乾隆纪实》等。

1793 年,英王乔治三世派马戛尔尼出使中国觐见乾隆帝,这无疑是当时的中英关系乃至中西关系史上最具影响力的外交活动。使团成员近 700 人,由物理学家、天文学家、美术学家、哲学家、技师、翻译以及舰队官员、水手、跟役等组成,他们带上了当时世界上最先进的天体运行仪、地球仪、枪炮、望远镜、秒表、试探气候架、火镜、军舰模型等作为礼品,以及英王乔治三世致乾隆的信,在正使马戛尔尼的带领下于 1792 年 10 月从英国出发,经历 10 个月的艰难航行后于 1793 年 6 月 19 日抵达中国海岸。斯当东担任此次访华使团的副使,他将沿途的所见所闻详细记载下来,写成《英使谒见乾隆纪实》一书。

《英使谒见乾隆纪实》详细记述了使团从派遣缘起,筹备工作,到使团出发经大西洋和赤道线,过大西洋南部和印度洋,访问爪哇岛,接近澳门,穿过黄海往天津,抵达中国首都北京,在避暑山庄谒见乾隆帝后返回国的全部经过。英国派遣这个使团到中国的“公务旅行”实际上是为了商业目的,目的是想开辟在中国的市场,满足当时英国社会中最活跃、最富裕的商人阶层的利益。1793 年的中国,正值乾隆盛世,清朝仍然处于疆域辽阔、人口众多、经济繁荣带来的自给自足状态，沉浸在天朝大国的故梦中。而只有22万平方公里的英国，人口不足1000万，经过工业革命后飞速发展成为新的海上霸主和初露锋芒的帝国之星。

在中英两方就使团成员是否必须在乾隆皇帝面前行三跪九叩之礼(即“礼仪之争”)而相互较劲之后，马戛尔尼使团在热河行宫两次谒见乾隆皇帝。不料，乾隆帝断然拒绝英国提出互设使馆、给予英国商人自由贸易、给英国商品进口税特别优惠等要求，并在给英王乔治三世的回信中留下传世名言：“天朝物产丰盈，无所不有，原不藉外夷货物以通有无。”

马戛尔尼使团一无所获离开中国，这是中英两个傲慢的帝国互相碰撞的结果，从此埋下了欧洲人以武力打开中国大门的伏笔。48年后，大英帝国的坚船利炮打开了古老中国的大门，揭开了中国近代史的篇章。

二、作品选读

Episode Ⅰ

The party, thus obliged to defer their return to the Lion, went to view the city or walled town of Ting-hai, situated within a mile from the large open village or suburb, built along the shore. The way from one to the other was over a plain, intersected with rivulets and canals in various directions, which possibly might serve, among other purposes, for that of separating the different properties of individuals. The ground was cultivated like a garden; not a single spot was waste; and the road, tho good, was narrow, as if in order that as little land as possible should be lost to culture.

The city walls were thirty feet high, and, like those of a large prison, overtopped the houses which they surrounded. Along the walls, at the distance of every hundred yards, were square stone towers. In the parapets were also embrasures, and holes in the merlons for archery; but there were no cannon, except a few old wrought-iron pieces near the gate. The gate was double; within which was a guard-house, where military men were stationed; and the bows and arrows, pikes, and matchlocks, orderly arranged, were, no doubt, intended for their use.

Of the towns of Europe, Ting-hai bore the resemblance most of Venice, but on a smaller scale. It was, in some degree, surrounded, as well as intersected, by canals. The bridges thrown over them were steep, and ascended by steps, like the Rialto. The streets, which were no more than alleys or narrow passages, were paved with square flat stones; but the houses, unlike the Venetian buildings, were low, and mostly of one story. The attention, as to ornament, in these buildings was confined chiefly to the roofs, which, besides having the tiles that cover the rafters luted and plastered over, to prevent accidents from their falling in stormy weather, were contrived in such a form as to imitate the inward bend of the ridges and sides of canvas tents, or of the coverings of skins of animals or other flexible materials, effected by their weight; a form preferred, perhaps, after the introduction of more solid materials, in allusion to the modes of shelter to which the human race had, probably, recourse before the erection of regular dwelling houses. On the ridges of the roofs were uncouth figures of animals, and other decorations in clay, stone, or iron. The town was full of shops, containing, chiefly articles of clothing, food, and furniture, displayed to full advantage. Even coffins were painted in a variety of lively and contrasting colors. The smaller quadrupeds, including dogs, intended for food, were, as well as poultry, exposed alive for sale, as were fish in tubs of water, and eels in sand. The number of places where tin-leaf, and sticks of odoriferous wood were sold, for burning in their temples, indicated no slight degree of superstitious disposition in the people. Loose garments and trousers were worn by both sexes; but the men had hats of straw or cane which covered the head, their hair, except one long lock, being cut short or shaved; while the women had theirs entire, and plaited and coiled, becomingly, into a knot upon the crown of the head, as is sometimes seen on the female statues of antiquity.

…

Of most of the latter, even in the middle and inferior classes, the feet were unnaturally small, or rather truncated. They appeared as if the fore part of the foot had been accidentally cut off, leaving the remainder of the visual size, and bandaged like the stump of an amputated limb. They undergo, indeed, much torment, and cripple themselves in great measure, in imitation of ladies of higher rank, among whom it is there the custom to stop, by pressure, the growth of the ancle as well as foot from the earliest infancy; and leaving the great toe in its natural position, forcibly to bend the others, and retain them under the foot, till at length they adhere to, as if buried in the sole, and can no more be separated.

——**Excerpted from *An Authentic Account of an Embassy from the king of Great Britain to the Emperor of China*. 1797. Vol. (1): 419 - 422. London: W. Bulmer And Co.**

New Words and Expressions

defer [di'fɜː]vt. 使推迟;使延期 vi. 推迟;延期;服从

intersect [intə'sekt]vi. 相交; 交叉 vt. 横断; 横切;贯穿

rivulet ['rivjʊlit]n. 小溪; 小河

overtop [əʊvə'tɒp]vt. 超出;凌驾;高耸……之上 n. 马甲

parapet ['pærəpit]n. 栏杆;扶手;矮护墙

merlon ['mɜːlən]n. 城齿;枪眼与枪眼之间的墙壁

archery ['ɑːtʃəri]n. 箭术

cannon ['kænən]n. 大炮;加农炮;榴弹炮;机关炮 vt. 炮轰 vi. 炮轰;开炮

wrought-iron [rɔːt 'ɑiən]n. 锻铁; 熟铁

matchlock ['mætʃlɒk]n. 火绳枪;火绳

resemblance [ri'zembl(ə)ns]n. 相似;相似之处;相似物;肖像

ascend [ə'send]vi. 上升;登高;追溯 vt. 攀登;上升

ornament ['ɔːnəm(ə)nt]n. 装饰;教堂用品 vt. 装饰; 修饰

confine [kən'fain]n. 界限; 边界;约束;限制 vt. 限制;禁闭

rafter ['rɑːftə]n. 椽;筏夫(等于 raftsman) vt. 装椽于

lute [luːt; ljuːt]n. 琵琶 vt. 弹诗琴表达；用封泥封 vi. 弹诗琴

plaster [ˈplɑːstə]n. 石膏；灰泥；膏药 vt. 减轻；粘贴；涂以灰泥；敷以膏药；使平服

contrive [kənˈtraiv]vt. 设计；发明；图谋 vi. 谋划；设法做到

ridge [ridʒ]n. 山脊；山脉；屋脊 vt. 使成脊状；作垄 vi. 成脊状

canvas [ˈkænvəs]n. 帆布 vt. 用帆布覆盖；用帆布装备 adj. 帆布制的

allusion [əˈluːʒ(ə)n]n. 暗示；提及

recourse [riˈkɔːs]n. 求援；求助；[经] 追索权；依赖；救生索

erection [iˈrekʃ(ə)n]n. 勃起；建造；建筑物；直立

coffin [ˈkɒfin]n. 棺材；断送

quadruped [ˈkwɒdrʊped]n. [脊椎] 四足动物 adj. 有四足的

poultry [ˈpəʊltri]n. 家禽；家禽肉

odoriferous [ˌəʊdəˈrif(ə)rəs]adj. 臭的；散发气味的；芬芳的

superstitious [suːpəˈstiʃəs]adj. 迷信的；由迷信引起的

disposition [dispəˈziʃ(ə)n]n. 处置；[心理] 性情；[军] 部署；倾向

plait [plæt]n. 褶；辫状物 vt. 编织；把……编成辫(等于 pleat)；给……打褶

coil [kɒil]vt. 盘绕；把……卷成圈 n. 线圈；卷 vi. 成圈状

truncate [trʌŋˈkeit]adj. 截短的；被删节的 vt. 把……截短；缩短；使成平面

bandage [ˈbændidʒ]n. 绷带 vt. 用绷带包扎

stump [stʌmp]n. 树桩；残余部分；假肢 vt. 砍伐；使为难 vi. 笨重地行走；发表竞选演说

amputate [ˈæmpjʊteit]vt. 截肢；切断；删除

Notes

1. The smaller quadrupeds, including dogs, intended for food, were, as well as poultry, exposed alive for sale, as were fish in tubs of water, and eels in sand(paragraph 3)：这里的 as 用作连词，表示也……一样。

如：She is a doctor, as was her husband.

她是一名医生，她的丈夫也是。

2. While the women had theirs entire, and plaited and coiled, becomingly, into a knot upon the crown of the head, as is sometimes seen on the female statues of antiquity(paragraph 3):这里的 as 用作关系代词，引导非限制性定语从句，用来指代它前面的整个句子(即先行句)，意思是"这一点"。这个分句可以位于句首、句中或句末。

如:(1) As is well known, oceans cover more than 70% of the earth.

我们知道，海洋占地球面积的百分之七十以上。

(2) As we all know, the earth goes around the sun.

众所周知，地球绕着太阳转。

Episode Ⅱ

The weather in the evening was favorable for departure; and the several yachts and other vessels belonging to, or connected with, the Embassy, sailed a little way beyond Tien-sing. It appeared, as the vessels passed through it, to be of considerable length. Some of the observers supposed it to extend as far as from Millbank to Lime-house, or about the length of London. The mandarins of the place asserted that its population was equal to seven hundred thousand souls. The immense number of spectators it supplied rendered such a computation likely, even allowing for the accession of persons from the neighborhood, whom the novel sight might have attracted ; but adding, at the same time, the due proportion of females and of children, that had mixed but little in the crowd. The junks, which were numerous enough almost to cover the waters which divide this commercial city, contained several thousand people. It is not alone to the persons sufficient to navigate those vessels that they afforded habitations. The wives and families of the officers and sailors reside with them constantly on board. There many of them are born; and all of them spend their lives. Every shore to them was foreign and the earth an element on which they ventured but occasionally.

Such of the houses of Tien-sing as, by having shops for the retail of merchandize, or working places for manufacturers, were open to the street, seemed as full of people as the habitations upon the water. Of the numbers contained in the other buildings some judgment may be formed, not only by those of the spectators seen abroad, but from the constant and, probably, patriarchal usage, to which this people still adhere, of having all the branches or existing generations of the same family, under a single roof, and in small apartments. In consequence of such usage, retained by the Chinese emigrants at Batavia, it appeared upon a regular census taken of the inhabitants of that settlement, that ten men fit to bear arms were found in every Chinese house.

The houses of Tien-sing were chiefly built of brick, of a leaden blue color. Few were red. Such as were used in the smallest and poorest dwellings, were of a pale brown. These different tints are supposed to have arisen not from any difference in the nature of the earth of which they severally consisted, but in the method of converting that earth into bricks. Those last mentioned had been exposed to no other heat than that of the sun, in which they were only baked or indurated imperfectly. The blue bricks were exposed to the action of a close wood fire, in kilns erected for that purpose, and where little actual flame was suffered to attain the surface of the bricks. Such as received the action of the flame were inclined to red. When the clay is first moulded into the form intended for bricks, it is the custom in the East to lay them at once in rows one above another. They are, when thus laid, in a soft and humid state, and from the nature of argillaceous earth, particularly adhesive. It becomes, therefore, in that state, necessary to keep them separated by some substance of a nature that will not itself adhere to either surface; without which the different rows of bricks would, as they dried, form together one solid mass, incapable of being applied to the use for which they were destined. This purpose is answered by placing between these rows thin layers of straw ; and this precaution is deemed so essential, that it has given rise to the oriental proverb, on this subject, which has passed into the languages of the west.

Many of the houses at Tien-sing are two stories high. This is contrary to the general mode which the Chinese affect in building. They mostly prefer houses of a single story, in conformity to the original form of all dwellings: and there are many Chinese who still feel awkwardly in ascending stairs, or looking down from heights. But the advantage of being near the quays and water side of a commercial town, has given rise to what is considered in that country as a duplication of building on the same site.

...

The Barbadoes millet was frequently planted in alternate rows, having between them rows of a smaller grain and humbler stems, either the panicum italicum, or panicum cms galli, to be sheltered for a time by its taller neighbor, until the latter shall be reaped; when the former, then fully exposed to the sun's rays, ripens in its turn, and is fitted for the sickle. Sometimes in small spots accidentally vacant near the edges of the bank, or along ridges of corn, was planted a species of dolichos, not unlike the kidney-bean. Sometimes were seen whole fields of beans, and also several of sesamum, and other plants, of which the seeds yield oil much used for culinary purposes. No weeds were any where observed to diminish useful produce, or to share with it the fruitfulness of the earth. Every field had the neatness and regularity of a garden. The corn and pulse then growing had succeeded to a former crop in the same year. Wheat in dry, and rice in moist, situations, were said to be cultivated to advantage.

Few trees or cattle adorn these plains. The eye, however, was delighted with the unbounded prospect of habitations, and the prosperous effect of careful culture. Famines sometimes happen, notwithstanding, in this part of the province. In some seasons inundations, produced by torrents from the mountains, and as often the depredations of locusts, are causes of this disaster. On these occasions, robberies are frequent; and, tho checked, are not easily repressed, by all the rigor and exertions of the government. But as they are, in fact, committed from necessity and the goadings of hunger, so they usually cease at the return of plenty.

——**Excerpted from *An Authentic Account of an Embassy from the king of Great Britain to the Emperor of China*. 1797. Vol. (2): 39 – 45. London: W. Bulmer And Co.**

New Words and Expressions

yacht[jɒt]vi. 乘游艇；驾游艇 n. 游艇，快艇；轻舟

spectator [spek'teitə]n. 观众；旁观者

render ['rendə]vt. 致使；提出；以……回报 vi. 给予补偿 n. 打底；交纳；粉刷

computation [kɒmpju'teiʃ(ə)n]n. 估计；计算

accession [ək'seʃ(ə)n]n. 增加；就职；到达 vt. 登记入册

reside [ri'zaid]vi. 住；居住；属于

patriarchal [peitri'ɑ:k(ə)l]adj. 家长的；族长的；由族长统治的

census ['sensəs]vt. 实施统计调查 n. 人口普查；人口调查

tint [tint]n. 色彩；浅色 vt. 染(发)；给……着色

convert [kən'vɜ:t]vt. 使转变；转换……；使……改变信仰 vi. 转变，变换；皈依 n. 皈依者

indurate ['indjʊreit]vt. 使硬化；使坚固 adj. 冷酷的；顽固的；硬化的 vi. 硬化

kiln [kiln]vt. 烧窑；在干燥炉干燥 n. (砖，石灰等的)窑；炉；干燥炉

mould [məʊld]vi. 发霉 vt. 浇铸；用泥土覆盖 n. 模具；霉

argillaceous [ˌɑ:dʒi'leiʃəs]adj. 黏土的[土壤]；含黏土的；似黏土的

precaution [pri'kɔ:ʃ(ə)n]n. 预防；警惕；预防措施 vt. 警惕；预先警告

quay [ki:]n. 码头

duplication [dju:pli'keiʃn]n. 复制；副本；成倍

millet ['milit]n. 小米；粟；稷；黍的籽实

stem [stem]n. 干；茎；船首；血统 vt. 阻止；除去……的茎；给……装柄 vi. 阻止

panicum ['pænikəm]n. 黍

sickle ['sik(ə)l]n. 镰刀

dolichos ['doli tʃɔ s]n. 扁豆

kidney-bean ['kidn bi:n]n. 菜豆；四季豆；肾形豆

culinary ['kʌlin(ə)ri]adj. 厨房的；烹调用的

adorn [ə'dɔ:n]vt. 装饰；使生色

inundation [inʌn'deiʃn]n. 洪水；泛滥

depredation [depri'deiʃ(ə)n]n. 掠夺；破坏；破坏痕迹

locust ['ləʊkəst]n. 蝗虫；蚱蜢

rigour ['rigə]n. 严格；严厉；苛刻；精确

goad [gəʊd]n. 刺激；(赶牲口用的)刺棒；激励 vt. 刺激；激励；煽动

Notes

1. Every shore to them was foreign and the earth an element on which they ventured but occasionally(paragraph 1)：此外"but"作副词，意思接近于 only，意为"只不过"。

如：(1) She is but a young girl.

她只不过是一个小女孩儿。

(2) She is but a liar.

她只不过是个说谎者。

2. Such as were used in the smallest and poorest dwellings, were of a pale brown(paragraph 3)：这里的 such as 表示"凡是……的人(或事物)""所有……的人(事物)"，其意相当于 everything that, all those, those that (who)等。其中的 such 为先行词，as 为关系代词。

如：(1) Take such (things) as you need.

你需要什么就拿什么。

(2)You may choose such as you prefer.

你可挑选自己想要的东西。

Episode Ⅲ

On his entrance into the tent he mounted immediately the throne by the front steps, consecrated to his use alone. Ho-choong-taung, and two of the principal persons of his household, were close to him, and always spoke to him upon their knees. The princes of his family, the tributaries and great officers of state being already arranged in their respective places in the tent, the president of the tribunal of rites conducted the Embassador, who was attended by his page and Chinese interpreter, and accompanied by the Minister Plenipotentiary, near to the foot of the throne, on the left hand side, which according to the usages of China, so often the reverse of those of Europe, is accounted the place of honor. The other gentlemen of the Embassy, together with a great number of mandarins and officers of inferior dignity, stood at the great opening of the tent, from whence most of the ceremonies that passed within it, could be observed.

…

The broad mantle, which as a Knight of the Order of the Bath the Embassador was entitled to wear, was somewhat upon the plan of dress most pleasing to the Chinese. Upon the same principles, the Minister Plenipotentiary, being an Honorary Doctor of Laws of the University of Oxford, wore the scarlet gown of that degree, which happened also to be suitable in a government where degrees in learning lead to every kind of political situation. The Embassador, instructed by the president of the tribunal of rites, held the large and magnificent square box of gold, adorned with jewels, in which was enclosed his Majesty's letter to the Emperor, between both hands lifted above his head ; and in that manner ascending the few steps that led to the throne, and bending on one knee, presented the box, with a short address, to his Imperial Majesty; who, graciously receiving the same with his own hands, placed it by his side, and expressed "the satisfaction he felt at the testimony which his Britannic Majesty gave to him of his esteem and good will, in sending him an Embassy, with a letter, and rare presents; that he, on his part, entertained sentiments of the same kind towards the sovereign of Great Britain, and hoped that harmony should always be maintained among their respective subjects."

This mode of reception of the representative of the King of Great Britain, was considered by the Chinese court, as particularly honorable and distinguished: Embassadors being seldom received by the Emperor on his throne, or their credentials delivered by them into his own hands, but into that of one of his courtiers. These distinctions, so little material in themselves, were however understood by this refined people as significant of a change in the opinions of their government in respect to the English; and made a favorable impression upon their minds.

His Imperial Majesty, after a little more conversation with the Embassador, gave, as the first present from him to his Majesty, a gem, or precious stone, as it was called by the Chinese, and accounted by them of high value. It was upwards of a foot in length, and curiously carved into a form intended to resemble a sceptre, such as is always placed upon the Imperial throne, and is considered as emblematic of prosperity and peace.

The Chinese etiquette requiring that Embassadors should, besides the presents brought in the name of the sovereign, offer others on their own part, his Excellency, and the Minister, or as the Chinese called him, the inferior Embassador, respectfully presented theirs; which his Imperial Majesty condescended to receive, and gave in return others to them. Those presents were probably, on both sides, less valuable in the estimation of the receivers than in that of the donors; but were mutually acceptable, upon the consideration of being tokens of respect on the one part, and of favor and good will upon the other.

During the ceremonies, his Imperial Majesty appeared perfectly unreserved, cheerful, and unaffected. The frontispiece to the first volume of this work, is a portrait of him, from a drawing by Mr. Alexander, one of the draughtsmen to the Embassy. It was made under unfavorable circumstances; yet the person, dress, and manner, are perfectly like the original; but the features of the face, which were taken by stealth, and at a glance, bear a less strong resemblance. This, of all the drawings made by Mr. Alexander throughout the route, the gentlemen of the Embassy, who had an opportunity of comparing them with the originals, thought the only one which was defective. To the facility and truth with which he caught with his pencil the most striking objects, and costume of the country, as the Embassy passed rapidly along, this work is principally indebted for the ornamental part of it, in which every plate is a faithful copy after nature.

To render the portrait of his Imperial Majesty more correct, it might have been proper to draw the eye more full and clear, and the countenance more open and cheerful. Such at least it was during the interview with the Embassador, which was lengthened by interpreting whatever was said by either party.

His Imperial Majesty, adverting to the inconvenience arising from such a circumstance, inquired from Ho choong-taung, whether any person of the Embassy understood the Chinese language; and being informed that the Embassador's page, a boy then in his thirteenth year, had alone made some proficiency in it, the Emperor had the curiosity to have the youth brought up to the throne, and desired him to speak Chinese. Either what he said, or his modest countenance, or manner, was so pleasing to his Imperial Majesty, that he took from his girdle a purse, hanging from it for holding areca nut, and presented it to him.

——**Excerpted from *An Authentic Account of an Embassy from the king of Great Britain to the Emperor of China*. 1797. Vol. (2): 229 – 234. London: W. Bulmer And Co.**

New Words and Expressions

consecrate ['kɒnsikreit]vt. 奉献;使神圣;供神用;献身于 adj. 神圣的

tributary ['tribjʊt(ə)ri]adj. 纳贡的;附属的;辅助的 n. 支流;进贡国;附属国

tribunal [trai'bjuːn(ə)l]n. 法庭;裁决;法官席

rite [rait]n. 仪式;惯例; 习俗;典礼

whence [wens]n. 根源 adv. 从何处 pron. 何处 conj. 由此

enclosed [in'klozd]adj. 被附上的;与世隔绝的

credential [kri'denʃ(ə)l]n. 证书;凭据;国书

courtier ['kɔːtiə]n. 朝臣;奉承者;谄媚者

sceptre ['septə]vt. 授予王权;拥登王位 n. 权杖;王权

emblematic [emblə'mætik]adj. 象征的;可当标志的

etiquette [ˈetiket; etiˈket]n. 礼节; 礼仪;规矩

sovereign [ˈsɒvrin]adj. 至高无上的;有主权的 n. 君主;独立国;最高统治者

condescend [kɒndiˈsend]vi. 屈尊;俯就;(对某人)表现出优越感

token [ˈtəʊk(ə)n]n. 表征;代币;记号 adj. 象征的;表意的 vt. 象征;代表

frontispiece [ˈfrʌntispiːs]n. 卷头插画;标题页 vt. 为书加卷首插图

draughtsmen [ˈdrɑːf(t)smən]n. 起草人;制图员;跳棋棋子

countenance [ˈkaʊnt(ə)nəns]n. 面容; 表情;支持 vt. 支持; 赞同

advert [ˈædvɜːt]vi. 注意;谈到 n. 广告

proficiency [prəˈfiʃ(ə)nsi]n. 精通; 熟练

三、思考题

1. 如何理解一些学者所说马戛尔尼出使中国的事件,结果“导致中国则与当时正处于雏形的‘WTO’失之交臂”?

2. 政治家拿破仑在评价马戛尔尼出使中国遭遇的所谓“礼仪之争”时,他认为外国使臣没有权利按照自己的习俗给出使国行礼,而必须按照出使国的习俗给出使国行礼,他甚至用了一个粗俗的说法来阐明这个道理:“如果英国的习俗不是吻国王的手,而是吻他的屁股,是否也要中国皇帝脱裤子呢?”你同意拿破仑的观点吗?

第五章

中华帝国纪行

一、作品导读

古伯察(Évariste-Régis Huc,1813—1860),法国遣使会传教士,同时也是一位精通汉语、满语、蒙语和少许藏语,学识渊博,熟悉中国经典著作的著名汉学家。古伯察 1839 年进入中国,曾旅居和游历澳门、广州、内蒙古、西藏、湖北、江西等地,他广泛接触了中国上至皇帝、大臣和王公贵族,下至普通百姓,对当时中国社会的政治、经济、文化、教育、文学等做了详细考察。著作有《鞑靼西藏旅行记》《中华帝国纪行》《基督教在中国、鞑靼和西藏》等,其中《鞑靼西藏旅行记》记录了他 1846 年在西藏的旅行见闻,出版后获得巨大成功,被翻译成英、德、荷兰、西班牙、意大利、瑞典、俄等多种文字。

《中华帝国纪行》是古伯察一部比《鞑靼西藏旅行记》更有趣,也更重要的作品,记录了他穿越中国整个心脏地区——从西藏边界到广东的旅行,该书涵盖了 19 世纪中期中国封建社会生活的方方面面,对上至清朝官场、下至汉族和其他少数民族在内的平民百姓的生活状况和心理状态作了细致而深刻的剖析,他对中国社会和文化的洞察力令人惊讶、令人佩服。

古伯察先后在中国各地旅行的经历长达 14 年之久,他在写作中国旅行见闻时,既克服了当时来华欧洲人怀有的"欧洲文化中心论"的情绪,也克服了当时西方人看待中国社会时普遍存在的赞扬或贬低的二元对立观点,他有时站在欧洲人的立场,有时候站在中国人的立场,力求用客观的态度去观察和评价中国。如古伯察对中国人吸食鸦片带来严重后果的看法,一方面他站在正义的立场谴责英国方面用鸦片伤害中国人的罪恶行径;另一方面也指出是腐败的清政府官员不争气让英国人钻了空子,因为英国商人的货船不仅受到英国政府的保护，也受到中国政府官员的保护。又如，他对中国的机构与政府进行深入探讨后，认为不应该对中国的专制政治加以痛骂，也不应当对父权制的智慧大唱赞歌。在古伯察的眼中，当时的中国仍然有许多值得赞扬的地方，如他在四川的旅行中发现中国农村基层普选制在当时世界上其他任何地方都没有那么完善；在四川考察了私塾教学之后，他认为中国教育非常自由，中国的初等教育方面肯定是世界上最普及的国家。

以下节选的是古伯察从西藏到四川途中旅行见闻文章。

二、作品选读

Episode Ⅰ

Two years had passed since we bade adieu to the Christians of the Valley of Black Waters. With the exception of a residence of some months in the Lama convent of Koumboum, and in the bosom of the capital of Buddhism, we had been since then perpetually journeying through the vast deserts of Tartary and over the high mountains of Tibet. But these two years of inexpressible fatigue were not sufficient; we were still far from the end of our sufferings. Before we could hope to enjoy any repose, we had to cross the frontiers of China, and traverse this immense empire from west to east.

Formerly, upon our first entrance on the mission, we had traversed it throughout its entire extent from north to south; but that was secretly, by stealth along by paths and in darkness pretty much, in fact, in the fashion of bales of contraband goods.

Now our position was altogether different. We were to march openly in broad daylight, keeping the middle of the Imperial high road. Those mandarins, the very sight of whom used to throw us into a cold shiver, and who would have been so extremely happy to put us to the torture, if we had fallen into their hands, had now to make up their minds to serve us for an escort, and to overwhelm us with respect and politeness all along the road.

We were about to become acquainted, in China, with a civilization extremely unlike that of Europe, but not less complete in its kind. The climate, too, would be no longer the same, and the means of communication would be greatly superior to those of Tartary and Tibet.

No more fear of snow, and rocks, and precipices of wild beasts and robbers of the desert. An immense population, provisions in abundance, a richly varied, magnificent landscape, luxurious and agreeable, though sometimes whimsical habitations this was what we might look for during this new and long stage of our journey. We knew the Chinese, however, too well to feel quite at our ease in this altered position. Ki-chan had, indeed, given orders that we should be treated kindly, but, in fact, we were, after all, given up to the tender mercies of the mandarins. After having escaped a thousand dangers in the wild countries that we had just passed through, we felt no security that we were not to perish of hunger and privation in the very bosom of abundance and civilization, and we were convinced that our fate would greatly depend on the attitude we should assume from the beginning.

——Excerpted from *A Journey Through the Chinese Empire*. 1855. Vol. (1): 27 - 29. New York: Harper & Brothers.

New Words and Expressions

adieu [ə'dju:]n. 告别;辞行;再见;再会

residence ['rezid(ə)ns]n. 住宅;住处;居住

Buddhism ['bʊdiz(ə)m]n. 佛教

perpetually [pə'pɛtʃʊəli]adv. 永恒地;持久地

inexpressible [,inik'sprɛsəbl]adj. 不可言传的;难以形容的;不能用语

言表达的

fatigue [fə'ti:g]n. 疲劳，疲乏；杂役 vt. & vi. 疲劳 adj. 疲劳的

repose [ri'pəʊz]n. 休息；睡眠；静止 vt. 使休息 vi. 休息

frontier ['frʌntiə]n. 前沿；边界；国境 adj. 边界的；开拓的

traverse [trə'vɝs]n. 穿过；横贯；横木 vt. 穿过；反对 vi. 横越；旋转

stealth [stɛlθ]n. 秘密；秘密行动；鬼祟

bypath ['bai, pæθ]n. 侧道；小路；私道

bale [bel]n. 包；捆；灾祸；不幸 v. 将…… 打包

contraband ['kɑntrə'bænd] n. 走私；走私货；战时禁运品（等于 contraband of war）

mandarin ['mændərin]n. （中国）普通话；国语；官话

acquaint [ə'kwent]vt. 使熟悉；使认识

superior [sə'piriər]adj. 上级的；优秀的 n. 上级；长官；优胜者

precipice ['prɛsəpis]n. 悬崖；绝壁；险境

provision [prə'viʒn]n. 规定；条款；准备；供应品 vt. 供给……食物及必需品

whimsical ['wimzikl]adj. 古怪的；异想天开的；反复无常的

habitation [, hæbi'teʃən]n. 居住；住所

mercy ['mɝsi]n. 仁慈；宽容；怜悯；幸运

perish ['pɛriʃ]vt. 使麻木；毁坏 vi. 死亡；毁灭；腐烂；枯萎

privation [prai'veʃən]n. 贫困；丧失

Notes

1. Before we could hope to enjoy(paragraph 1)：before 在这里用作连词，意思是"在……之前；还没来得及 …… 就"。

如：(1) Before she could move, she heard a great noise, which grew to a terrible roar.

她还没来得及动弹，就听见有很响的声音，接着就成了可怕的隆隆轰鸣声。

(2) Before I could say a word, she had stormed out of the room.

不等我说一句话，她就冲出了房间。

(3) Don't count your chickens before they are hatched.

不要高兴得过早。

2. Those mandarins, the very sight of whom used to throw us into a cold shiver, and who would have been so extremely happy to put us to the torture, if we had fallen into their hands, had now to make up their minds to serve us for an escort, and to overwhelm us with respect and politeness all along the road(paragraph 3):这是一个比较复杂的句子结构。句子主要结构是 Those mandarins had now to make up their minds to serve us for an escort, and to overwhelm us with respect... the very sight of whom used to throw us into a cold shiver, and who... 是分别由 whom 和 who 引导的非限制性定语从句,用于修饰主语 those mandarins。if we had fallen into their hands 是一个 if 引导的条件状语从句,表示虚拟。这里的 had fallen 表示与过去事实相反。这种表示与过去事实相反的常用结构为:had + 过去分词。

如:He would be more successful if he had taken his father's advice in the early days.

如果他早听了他父亲的意见,他就会更成功。

Episode Ⅱ

The road that we had been following from Ta-tsien-lou had been constantly descending, and we soon found ourselves in a deep and narrow valley, watered by a limpid stream, whose banks were fringed by willows and bamboos. On either side arose, almost perpendicularly, lofty and majestic mountains, ornamented with stately trees, and an inexhaustible variety of plants and flowers. Our eyes feasted on the brilliant colors, and the exquisite verdure, and were filled with tears of delight as we inhaled the balmy fragrance of the air: our whole being seemed to expand with rapture. One must have lived for two whole years amidst ice and snow, dreary arid mountains and sandy deserts to feel all the intoxicating charm of such a landscape, and the delicious repose afforded by fresh green grass to an eye wearied by the dead, monotonous whiteness of snow.

The road led along the course of the stream. Sometimes we passed from one bank to the other over little wooden bridges covered with turf, and sometimes over large stones thrown into the bed of the rivulet. But nothing relaxed the speed of our bearers; on they went, over every obstacle, and always with the same rapidity, agility, and courage. Now and then they made a short halt to wipe the sweat from their brows and smoke a pipe, and then they resumed their march with redoubled vigor. The narrow valley we were passing through seemed but little frequented; we met only from time to time some parties of travelers, among whom it was easy for us to distinguish the vigorous, energetic, and barbarous Tibetan from the pallid, cunning-looking faces of the civilized Chinese. On all sides we could see flocks of goats and long-haired oxen, feeding on the mountain pastures, while countless birds warbled amidst the branches of the trees. We passed the first night in an humble and badly provided inn but as the habitations we had met with in Tibet had not accustomed us to much luxury, we were very well pleased with what we found. The miseries of every kind that we had suffered, had had the effect of rendering us patient under all the trials of life.

On the following day, the road became more wild and perilous. As we advanced, the valley closed in, and became encumbered with enormous masses of rock and great trees that had fallen from the crest of the mountains. The stream that had borne us company the day before, like a faithful friend, now gradually turned away from us, and at last disappeared in a deep gorge. A torrent that we had heard roaring for a long time, like distant thunder, suddenly came in sight from behind a mountain and dashed itself furiously over the rocks. We followed it a long time in its erratic course, and saw it descend from point to point in noisy cascades, or trail its greenish waters like a huge serpent into dark hollows of the mountains. On this day we had no longer the pleasure of gazing on a peaceful and smiling landscape of trees and flowers, but this wild and savage grandeur of nature was not without its charms.

——**Excerpted from *A Journey Through the Chinese Empire*. 1855. Vol. (1). 33 – 35. New York: Harper & Brothers.**

New Words and Expressions

descend [di'sɛnd]vi. 下降；下去；下来；遗传；屈尊　vt. 下去；沿……向下

limpid ['limpid]adj. 透明的；平静的；无忧虑的

fringe [frindʒ]n. 边缘；穗；刘海　adj. 边缘的；附加的　vt. 加穗于

perpendicularly [pəːpən'dikjuləli]adv. 垂直地；直立地

majestic [mə'dʒɛstik]adj. 庄严的；宏伟的

ornament ['ɔrnəmənt]n. 装饰；教堂用品　vt. 装饰；修饰

inexhaustible [inig'zɔstəbl]adj. 用不完的；不知疲倦的

feast [fist]vt. & vi. 享受；款待；宴请　n. 筵席

exquisite [ik'skwizit]adj. 精致的；细腻的；优美的；高雅的

verdure ['vɝdjə˞]n. 碧绿

balmy ['bɑmi]adj. 芳香的；温和的；止痛的

fragrance ['fregrəns]n. 香味；芬芳

rapture ['ræptʃə˞]n. 兴高采烈 vt. 使……狂喜

amidst [ə'midst] prep. 在…当中

dreary ['driri]adj. 沉闷的；枯燥的

arid ['ærid]adj. 干旱的；不毛的；荒芜的

intoxicating [in'tɒksikeitiŋ]adj. 醉人的；令人陶醉的

repose [ri'poz]n. 休息；睡眠；静止 vt. & vi. 休息；依靠

weary ['wiəri]adj. 疲倦的；厌烦的；令人厌烦的 vt. & vi. 疲倦；厌烦

turf [tɜːf]n. 草皮；泥炭；跑马场 vt. 覆草皮于

rivulet ['rivjʊlit]n. 小溪；小河

agility [ə'dʒiləti]n. 敏捷；灵活；机敏

barbarous ['bɑːb(ə)rəs]adj. 野蛮的；残暴的

pallid ['pælid]adj. 苍白的；暗淡的；无生气的

pasture ['pɑːstʃə]n. 草地；牧场；牧草 vt. 放牧；吃草

warble ['wɔːb(ə)l]n. 鸟啭鸣；颤声 vt. & vi. 鸟鸣；用柔和的颤声唱

habitation [hæbi'teiʃ(ə)n]n. 居住；住所

render ['rendə]vt. 致使；提出；实施 vi. 给予补偿 n. 交纳；粉刷

perilous [ˈperiləs]adj. 危险的；冒险的

encumber [inˈkʌmbə]vt. 阻塞；妨害；拖累

crest [krest]n. 波峰；冠；山顶 vi. 到达绝顶；形成浪峰

borne [bɔːn]v. 忍受；负荷；结果实；生子女(bear 的过去分词)

gorge [gɔːdʒ]n. 峡谷；胃；暴食；咽喉 vt. & vi. 吃饱；吞下；使扩张

torrent [ˈtɔrənt]n. 奔流；倾注；迸发；连续不断

erratic [iˈrætik]adj. 不稳定的；古怪的 n. 漂泊无定的人；古怪的人

cascade [kæsˈkeid]n. 小瀑布；瀑布状物；串联 vi. & vi. 像瀑布般大量倾泻下来

serpent [ˈsəːp(ə)nt]n. 蛇(尤指大蛇或毒蛇)；狡猾的人

savage [ˈsævidʒ]adj. 野蛮的；残酷的 n. 未开化的；粗鲁的人；残暴成性的人

Notes

1. ...and we soon found ourselves in a deep and narrow valley, watered by a limpid stream(paragraph 1)：本句用到了 find 的复合结构 find ＋宾语＋宾语补足语，其中宾语补足语可以是名词、代词、形容词、副词、介词短语、省略 to 的不定式、v-ing 或过去分词来充当。

如：(1) She found a wallet lying on the ground.

她发现地上有一个钱包。

(2)He found the place much changed.

他发现那地方变化不小。

(3)He was found dead in the morning.

早上，有人发现他死了。

2. On either side arose, almost perpendicularly, lofty and majestic mountains, ornamented with stately trees, and an inexhaustible variety of plants and flowers(paragraph 1)：在英语中，主语和谓语的语序通常是主语在前、谓语在后，但有时由于语法或修辞的需要将谓语的部分或全部提到主语前面，这样的语序叫作倒装。整个谓语移至主语前面叫完全倒装。只把助动词、系动词或情态动词放在主语之前叫部分倒装。On either side arose...lofty and majestic mountains 属于完全倒装句，谓语 arose 移到主语

lofty and majestic mountains之前，起到强调的作用。

Episode Ⅲ

In a very long journey, some change in the mode of traveling is always desirable, as the uniformity becomes at last excessively wearisome; the palanquin has, doubtless, its advantages, which are not to be despised; but to be for a long time together shut up every day in a cage, and balanced upon the shoulders of four unfortunate fellows, whom you see panting, and perspiring with heat and fatigue one does, sometimes, get rather tired of that.

We proposed, therefore, to our conductors to make a stage by water; the proposal was received with enthusiasm, and, for fear we should change our minds, everybody made as much haste as possible in preparing for the embarkation: as they knew that we had a horror of dawdling, they displayed a really marvelous activity. According to our recommendation, two boats were hired, one for ourselves and the Mandarins, the other for the soldiers, attendants, and palanquin bearers; and as soon as ever we came on board they weighed anchor, and we set off, the beauty of the weather and the calmness of the water affording us hopes of a pleasant journey. The cabin we occupied was spacious, and pretty well ventilated; and if not absolutely clean, was at least tolerably dirty.

…

Their repertoire appeared inexhaustible, and, now they had once begun, we had great difficulty in inducing them to resume a language and manners more in accordance with their official dignity. To say the truth, however, our Mandarins really only wanted a little more practice, and a rather better memory, to make excellent actors. There is, perhaps, not a people in the world who carry so far their taste and passion for theatrical entertainments as the Chinese. We said just now that they were a nation of cooks, and we might also assert, with truth, that they are a nation of actors. These men have minds and bodies endowed with so much suppleness and elasticity, that they can transform themselves at will, and express by turns the most opposite passions. There is, in fact, a good deal of the monkey in their nature, and, when one has lived some time among them, one can not but wonder how people in Europe could ever take it into their heads that China was a kind of vast academy, peopled with sages and philosophers. Their gravity and their wisdom, exclusive of some official proceedings, are scarcely found out of their classical books. The Celestial Empire has much more resemblance to an immense fair, where, amidst a perpetual flux and reflux of buyers and sellers, of brokers, loungers, and thieves, you see in all quarters stages and mountebanks, jokers and comedians, laboring uninterruptedly to amuse the public. Over the whole surface of the country, in the eighteen provinces, in the towns of the first, second, and third order, in the burghs and the villages, rich and poor, Mandarins and people, all the Chinese, without exception, are passionately addicted to dramatic representations. There are theatres every-where; the great towns are full of them, and the actors play night and day. There is no little village that has not its theatre, which is usually placed opposite to the pagoda, and sometimes even forms a part of it. In some circumstances the permanent theatres are not found sufficient, and then the Chinese construct temporary ones, with wonderful facility, out of bamboo. The Chinese theatre is always extremely simple, and its arrangements are such as to exclude all idea of scenic illusion. The decorations are fixed, and do not change as long as the piece lasts. One would never know what they were intended for, if the actors themselves did not take care to inform the public, and correct the motionless character of the scenes by verbal explanations. The only arrangement that is ever made with a view to scenic effect is the introduction of a kind of trap-door in the front of the stage, that serves for the entrances and exits of supernatural personages, and goes by the name of the " Gate of Demons."

...

Our voyage on the Blue River was rapid and extremely pleasant. We arrived at Fou-ki-hien in the afternoon, having gone 150 li, or about 45 miles, in four hours and a half.

——**Excerpted from *A Journey Through the Chinese Empire*. 1855. Vol. (1): 270 - 276. New York: Harper & Brothers.**

New Words and Expressions

uniformity [juːniˈfɔːmiti]n. 均匀性;一致;同样

palanquin [pælənˈkiːn]n. 轿子;肩舆

fatigue [fəˈtiːg]n. 疲劳;疲乏;杂役 vt. 使疲劳;使心智衰弱 vi. 疲劳

embarkation [embaːˈkeiʃən]n. 从事;装载;乘坐

dawdling [ˈdɔdl]adj. 懒散的;闲逛的

anchor [ˈæŋkə]n. 锚;抛锚停泊;新闻节目主播 vt. 抛锚;使固定;主持节目

ventilate [ˈventileit]vt. 使通风;给……装通风设备;宣布

repertoire [ˈrepətwaː]n. 全部节目;计算机指令系统

suppleness [ˈsʌplnis]n. 柔软;易弯曲;顺从

elasticity [elæˈstisiti]n. 弹性;弹力;灵活性

flux [flʌks]n. 流量;变迁;不稳定;流出 vt. 使熔融;用焊剂处理

reflux [ˈriːflʌks]n. 逆流;退潮

mountebank [ˈmauntibæŋk]n. 江湖医生;江湖骗子 vi. 行骗

pagoda [pəˈgəʊdə]n. (东方寺院的)宝塔;印度的旧金币

trap-door n. 活板门;天窗

Notes

1. for fear we should change our minds, every body made as much haste as possible(paragraph 2): for fear that 可以用来引导虚拟语气,其形式通常为:"for fear that +主语+ should +动词原形"。句中的 should 可以省去。

如:I will not make a noise for fear that I (should) disturb you.

我不会作声的,以免打扰你。

2. The cabin we occupied was spacious, and pretty well ventilated; and if not absolutely clean, was at least tolerably dirty(paragraph 2): if not 可视为一个否定的条件状语从句省略。

如:(1) I might see you tomorrow. If not, then it'll be Saturday.

我可能明天去看你。如果不是明天，那就在周六。

(2)Ask her if it is a convenient time. If not, can she suggest another possible time?

问问她那个时间方便不方便。要是不方便，那她可不可以提出一个可行的时间?

注:有时 not 还可修饰另一个词语。

如:(1) If not today, tomorrow I'm sure you'll get an answer.

如果今天得不到回信，明天准能得到。

(2)This is one of the oldest buildings in town, if not the oldest.

这是城里最古老的房屋之一，如果不是最古老的话。

(3)Usually, if not always, we write "cannot" as one word.

我们即使不总是如此，也通常是把 cannot 作为一个词来拼写的。

3. These men have minds and bodies endowed with so much suppleness and elasticity(paragraph 3): have...endowed with 中 have 属于使役动词，句子结构常为" have + sth (宾语) + 过去分词(宾语补足语)"意为"让/叫/使/请别人做某事",宾语 sth 后面用过去分词作宾语补足语，说明 sth 与过去分词表示的动作之间是被动关系。

如:(1) We had the machine mended just now.

我们刚才请人把机器修好了。

(2)He has had his hair cut. 他(请人给他)理发了.

(3)The patient is going to have his temperature taken.

这个病人准备请/叫/让人量体温。

endowed with 意为"赋有、具有、赋予"等。

如:(1) Jane is endowed with many talents.

简多才多艺。

(2)He was endowed with the spirit of self-sacrifice.

他富有自我牺牲精神。

4. Mandarins and people, all the Chinese, without exception, are

passionately addicted to dramatic representations(paragraph 3): be addicted to 意思是“沉溺于，上瘾……”，后面常接名词或是动词的 ing 形式，是惯用用法。

如:(1) Many of the women are addicted to heroin and cocaine.

这些女人中很多人都吸食海洛因和可卡因成瘾了。

(2)I know a lot of people who are addicted to smoking.

我知道很多人吸烟上了瘾。

5. One would never know what they were intended for(paragraph 3): be intended for 意思是“用来……;为……而设定、准备”。

如:(1) The school to be built is intended for the disabled children.

即将要建的学校是为残疾儿童而设的。

(2) This book is intended for adults only.

这本书是为成年人而写的。

三、思考题

1. 古伯察是一位精通中国语言文化的学者,文本中哪些地方可以体现古伯察对中国人生活状况和心理状态所作的细致而深刻的剖析?

2. 古伯察对中国社会和文化的洞察力令人惊讶、令人佩服,如何理解他力求用客观的态度去观察和评价中国?

第六章

中国五十年见闻录

一、作品导读

阿奇博尔德·约翰·立德(Archibald John Little,1838—1908),英国商人、冒险家。立德1838年出生于伦敦,1859年来到中国,在德国人开办的洋行担任茶叶质检员,曾参加与太平军的作战被清朝授予从三品官衔。立德在中国生活近50年,他长期在四川居住,并开办了重庆贸易公司,打通了长江上游地区的贸易航线。在经商、游历中国的同时,立德对写作有浓厚的兴趣,多年来笔耕不辍,著有《穿越长江三峡》《峨眉山之游》《中国五十年见闻录》《远东》《云南之旅》等作品。1866年,立德当选为英国皇家地理学会会员。

《中国五十年见闻录》内容较为庞杂,收集了立德写于不同时期题为《两座城市:伦敦和北京》《中国纪行》《新路记述》《温泉游记》《激流新航与轮船首次抵渝》《长江上游历险记》《重访四川》《舟山群岛游记》等文章,是立德作为一个外国旅行者在中国多年见闻的集合,他在书中很多地方详细记载了旅途中的见闻感受,透露出作者对碰到的任何问题都感兴趣的作风。该书继承了作者之前《穿越长江三峡》和《峨眉山之游》深刻描写中国风土人情的传统,用生动幽默的语言将亲身经历娓娓道来,体现了作者深刻的洞察力,充满了真知与感悟。

需要指出的是,立德并非纯粹的学者,也不是一位高明的政治家,而是一位具有一定代表性的唯利是图的近代西方商人。《中国五十年见闻录》反映出像立德这样的近代西方人在殖民探险、殖民战争中踏上中国这片异域土地时持有的二重心态:即一方面极力赞扬中国古代文化,另一方面又以西方文化优越感的姿态抨击近代中国社会的落后。因此,《中国五十年见闻录》既有对中国美丽景色和传统文化的赞美，也有对当时中国落后、衰败的惋叹，是晚清时期西方人看中国文化游记的代表性作品。

二、作品选读

Episode Ⅰ

Our voyage up the rapids, starting on June 14, 1901, occupied roughly as many days as, at the same date the year before, the *Pioneer* occupied hours; thus to reach the big rapid, the " Yeh-tan", about 60 miles above Ichang, took us six days, as against the *Pioneer's* eight hours on June 12, 1900. We, on our third day out, passed the Tungling rapid, 35 miles distant from Ichang, on the rocks in which the *Sui-hsiang* was wrecked on the very morning of her departure from Ichang. This " pierced mountain " rapid is caused by the outflow from the Grand Mi-tan gorge passing through a nest of rocks, amidst which in winter the river forces its way in numerous winding channels. In June these rocks are deeply submerged, and only traceable by the boiling water as the 7-knot current sweeps over them. The long time spent by us in reaching this point was due to the difficulties of the "Yao-tsa-ho" below, as the winding reach, some 15 miles in length, which connects the Ichang and Mi-tan gorges, is called by the boatmen. The river valley here widens out, and whereas in the two gorges the stream has cut its way down through the limestone mountain, making itself a passage with vertical walls 1,000 to 2, 000 feet in height, in this connecting reach the river has to contend with a granitic formation, which it has disintegrated and broken up into piles of gigantic boulders, which lie strewn along the floor of the here widened valley in vast mounds such as none but Yangtze trackers, trained to them from childhood, would attempt to climb over. The points thus formed convert the Yao-tsa-ho into a continuous rapid, which the junk has to surmount without ever being able to gain a straight lead for its tow-lines ; hence a perpetual struggle, which the imperturbable Chinaman calmly accepts as all in the day's work, but which is most exasperating to the impatient foreigner. To the geologist this reach is peculiarly interesting as the one point in the navigable Yangtze at which igneous rocks lie athwart the river's course, and where a dyke of porphyry has been cut through by the stream.

Immediately above the Mi-tan gorge the valley, though still bounded by precipitous mountains rising to 3, 000 and 4, 000 feet, opens out, leaving a bench on either hand upon which are built the busy village of Hsin-tan (" New rapid") and the picturesque houses of prosperous farmers and junk-owners, forming a coup d'oeil that can hardly be excelled in any part of the world. Writing of the Hsin-tan as it appears in January, Mrs. Bishop remarks, " No description can convey an idea of the noise and turmoil of the Hsin-tan. I realized it best by my hearing being affected for some days afterwards. The tremendous crash and roar of the cataract, above which the yells and shouts of hundreds of straining trackers are heard, mingled with the ceaseless beating of drums and gongs, some as signals, others to frighten evil spirits, make up a pandemonium which can never be forgotten. "

——**Excerpted from *Gleanings from Fifty Years in China*. 1910:140 - 141. Philadelphia:J. B. Lippincott Company.**

New Words and Expressions

rapid ['ræpid]adj. 迅速的;险峻的 n. 急流;高速交通工具;高速交通网

wreck [rek]n. 破坏;残骸;失去健康的人 vt. 破坏;使失事;拆毁 vi. 失事

pierce [piəs]vt. 刺穿;洞察;响彻;深深地打动 vi. 进入;透入

gorge [gɔːdʒ]n. 峡谷;暴食;咽喉 vt. 使吃饱;吞下 vi. 拼命吃;狼吞虎咽

winding ['waindiŋ]n. 绕;缠;线圈;弯曲 adj. 弯曲的;蜿蜒的;卷绕的

submerge [səb'mɜːdʒ]vt. 淹没;把……浸入;沉浸 vi. 淹没;潜入水中;

湮没

traceable ['treisəbl]adj. 起源于；可追踪的；可描绘的

limestone ['laimstəʊn]n. 石灰岩

granitic [grə'nitik]adj. 花岗石的；由花岗岩形成的

disintegrate [dis'intigreit]vt. 使分解；使碎裂；使衰变 vi. 瓦解；碎裂；衰变

boulder ['bəʊldə]n. 卵石；大圆石；巨砾

strewn [struːn]v. 撒；散播(strew 的过去分词) adj. 撒满的；散播的

mound [maʊnd]n. 堆；高地；坟堆；护堤 vt. 堆起；筑堤 vi. 积成堆

surmount [sə'maʊnt]vt. 克服；越过；战胜

imperturbable [ˌimpə'təːbəb(ə)l]adj. 冷静的；泰然自若的

exasperate [ig'zæsp(ə)reit]vt. 恶化；使恼怒；激怒

navigable ['nævigəb(ə)l]adj. 可航行的；可驾驶的；适于航行的

igneous ['igniəs]adj. 火的；火成的；似火的

athwart [ə'θwɔːt]adv. 横跨着；相反 prep. 横跨；与……相反

dyke [daik]n. 堤；女子同性恋者

porphyry ['pɔːfiri]n. [岩] 斑岩

precipitous [pri'sipitəs]adj. 险峻的；急躁的；鲁莽的

coup [kuː]n. 政变；妙计；出乎意料的行动 vt. 使……倾斜 vi. 推倒；倾斜；溢出

turmoil ['təːmɒil]n. 混乱；骚动

cataract ['kætərækt]n. 白内障；大瀑布；暴雨；洪水；奔流 vt. 倾注

strain [stren]n. 应变；变形 v. 拉紧；竭尽……的全力；使……损坏

gong [gɒŋ]n. 锣；钟状物；奖章 vt. 鸣锣传唤 vi. 鸣锣

pandemonium [pændə'moniəm]n. 一片混乱；闹哄哄的场所

Notes

1. We, on our third day out, passed theTunghng rapid, 35 miles distant from Ichang, on the rocks in which the Sui-hsiang was wrecked on the very morning of her departure from Ichang(paragraph 1)：这里的 very 用作形容词，意为“正是”“恰是”，通常要与 the, this, that, my, your 等

连用。

如：(1) The very idea [thought].

真是个馊主意。

(2) You are the very man I want to see.

你正是我想要见的人。

(3) At that very moment the phone rang.

就在那时电话铃响了。

2. "The tremendous crash and roar of the cataract, above which the yells and shouts of hundreds of straining trackers are heard, mingled with the ceaseless beating of drums and gongs, some as signals, others to frighten evil spirits, make up a pandemonium which can never be forgotten."这里的 which 用作关系代词，引导非限制性定语从句，修饰先行词 the cataract。关系代词 which 在定语从句中作介词的宾语时，可以跟介词一起放在主句和从句之间，这时的关系代词不能省略；有时为了使关系代词紧跟它所修饰的先行词，也可以把介词放在从句中有关动词的后面。

如：This is the room in which he used to live. = This is the room (which/that) he used to live in.

这是他过去居住过的房间。

Episode Ⅱ

I left Cheng-tu by water in all the luxury of a " wupan " rowed down stream by four men, and though pleasant at first, I came to the conclusion, before twenty-four hours were over, that the confinement of a small boat was a bad exchange for the exercise and freedom of land travel, maugre its frequent discomforts. Yet the beautifully accidenté country, in all its spring bravery, red rocks, blue water, variegated blossoms, bamboos, dark forest trees, temples glittering with tiles of green and gold, elegant shimmer, rock carvings, Mantse caves, gorges and rapids, makes a panorama each turn in which is a picture that any artist might paint with pleasure.

In one respect the stretch of river 500 miles above Chungking and which gives water communication to the busy towns of Chang-peh-sha, Luchow, Sui-fu, Kia-ting, and Cheng-tu, affords a marked contrast to the 500 miles below Chungking. In this stretch, although still a rapid stream, the river follows the valleys in a natural way and runs parallel with the stratification ; hence there are no cross reefs athwart the current, and though races attended by whirlpools, dangerous to ill-found craft, occur, it is not a vicious river as is the stretch below. In the lower section the Yangtze has cut across the mountain ranges and runs at right angles to them and to the strata, its rebellious course giving rise to the many cross reefs which have produced the bad rapids, whirlpools, and Pao-tse which infest this section. Whether this perversity is due to the fact of this portion of the channel having been excavated by the Great Yü, I know not; but it seems not improbable, as the course chosen is in strict accordance with the orthodox rules that govern Chinese roadmaking.

A fortnight of panorama palls however by its very perfection, and I was heartily glad to set my foot once more on shore in Chungking, to feel myself in touch with the world, and above all to read the newspapers and learn the war news. In Cheng-tu we had had a bare telegram telling of Lord Roberts' advance to Bloemfontein, a happy surprise coming upon my latest previous news, that of the repulse at Spion kop on the 2nd February. Thus was Chungking reached (after a long two years' furlough in foreign parts), via Cheng-tu, in forty-seven days from Ichang, and at the end of a most interesting journey of nearly 1, 200 miles.

…

Knowing what doubtful characters many of these English-speaking Chinese are (Colquhoun's experience may be added to the above instances), would it not be well for exploring and surveying parties to engage the services of competent European interpreters? There are now some six hundred Protestant missionaries in Western China; should it not be possible to obtain the services of some who could be temporarily spared to aid in what is, after all, true Mission work ? A gentleman from the China Inland Mission accompanied Mrs. Bishop in her recent journeyings on the Tibetan border. I think myself that a consul should not be empowered to grant a passport for travel in the remote interior without an assurance that the applicant either speaks the language himself or is accompanied by an interpreter of some social standing. Had Captain Pottinger been accompanied by an intelligent interpreter, capable of reasoning with the people and explaining his objects, the regrettable incident would probably not have occurred and much ill-feeling thereby aroused against Europeans would have been avoided.

——**Excerpted from *Gleanings from Fifty Years in China*. 1910: 167 - 170. Philadelphia: J. B. Lippincott Company.**

New Words and Expressions

variegate ['veəriəgeit]vt. 使多样化;使丰富多彩;使成杂色

shimmer ['ʃimə]n. 微光;闪光 vi. 闪烁;发闪烁的微光 vt. 使闪烁

panorama [pænə'rɑːmə]n. 全景;全貌;全景画;概论

stratification [strætifi'keiʃən]n. 层理;成层

reef [riːf]n. 暗礁;矿脉;收帆 vt. & vi. 收帆;缩帆

athwart [ə'θwɔːt]adv. 横跨着;相反 prep. 横跨;与……相反

whirlpool ['wɜːlpuːl]n. 漩涡;涡流;混乱;纷乱

vicious ['viʃəs]adj. 恶毒的;恶意的;堕落的;有错误的;品性不端的

strata ['strɑːtə]n. 层;地层;阶层

rebellious [ri'beljəs]adj. 反抗的;造反的;难控制的

infest [in'fest]vt. 骚扰;寄生于;大批出没;大批滋生

perversity [pə'vɜːsiti]n. 邪恶;任性;性变态

excavate ['ekskəveit]vt. 挖掘;开凿 vi. 发掘;细查

orthodox ['ɔːθədɒks]adj. 正统的;传统的;惯常的;东正教的 n. 正统的人;正统的事物

panorama [pænə'rɑːmə]n. 全景;全貌;全景画;概论

pall [pɔːl]n. 幕;棺罩;遮盖物 vt. 覆盖;使乏味 vi. 走味

repulse [ri'pʌls]vt. 拒绝;驱逐;憎恶 n. 拒绝;击退

missionary ['miʃ(ə)n(ə)ri]adj. 传教的;传教士的 n. 传教

temporarily ['temp(ə)r(ər)ili]adv. 临时地；临时

consul ['kɒns(ə)l]n. 领事；(古罗马的)两执政官之一

empower [im'pɑʊə]vt. 授权，允许；使能够

Notes

1. In this stretch, although still a rapid stream, the river follows the valleys in a natural way and runs parallel with the stratification(paragraph 2)：这里的 run parallel with 意为“平行于；与……平行”。

如：The road runs parallel with the sea.

这条道路与海边平行。

2. Knowing what doubtful characters many of these English-speaking Chinese are (Colquhoun's experience may be added to the above instances), would it not be we for exploring and surveying parties to engage the services of competent European interpreters (paragraph 4)：这里的“knowing...”属于分词作状语，所表示的动作与句子主语构成逻辑上的主谓关系，用于修饰动词或者整个句子，可以表示时间、原因、条件、让步、结果、伴随、方式等。

如：(1) Hearing the news, she got frightened.

听到这个消息，她感到害怕。

(2)The boy ran even faster, reaching the school out of breath.

那个男孩跑得更快了，到达学校时累得上气不接下气了。

(3)Being a student, I must study hard.

作为一名学生，我必须努力学习。

3. Had Captain Pottinger been accompanied by an intelligent interpreter, capable of reasoning with the people and explaining his objects, the regrettable incident would probably not have occurred and much ill feeling thereby aroused against Europeans would have been avoided(paragraph 4)：这句是条件状语从句的虚拟语气。对过去的虚拟，had 提前，省掉 if，原句是：If Captain Pottinger had been accompanied by an intelligent interpreter, capable of reasoning with the people and explaining his objects, the regrettable incident would probably not have occurred and

much ill feeling thereby aroused against Europeans would have been avoided.

Episode Ⅲ

The stage in China, as we see it today, appears almost exactly identical with the stage in England in Shakespeare's time. The only pictorial representation that has come down to us of the Globe Theatre, Blackfriars, is by the Dutch traveler De Witte. There, as now in China, we see a stage composed of a square platform projecting into the pit, with a door of entrance and a door of exit on each side of the rear wall. There is a total absence of scenery, so that the whole weight of the performance falls upon the actors, who were doubtless as universally excellent in Shakespeare's time as they are today in China. The musicians are seated at the back of the stage in full view of the audience. And the wealthy patrons are seated in galleries round the open courtyard. It is particularly noticeable that the pit, in all theatrical representations in China, whether given in the courtyards of the temples, in the halls of the guilds, or in the houses of the rich, is always open free to the poor, a custom which I should not be sorry to see imitated in England today. In connection with this fact it is interesting to mention that, when travelling in China through the scenes rendered famous in song and history, I have been astonished at the accurate knowledge of the old wars and dynasties displayed by illiterate boatmen on the river and by our porters on land journeys. They are never tired of pointing out historic sites to the foreign traveler, and expatiating upon the great deeds of former generations. It was a long time before I could learn whence these men derived their knowledge, so far surpassing the acquaintance with history displayed by similar classes in our own country. I at last discovered that they had learnt their history in that pleasantest and most impressive of all schools, the Theatre. Elaborate historical dramas form the bulk of the performances given in the public theatre, which almost every village in China possesses, by companies of strolling players who are paid by subscriptions from the more wealthy inhabitants.

——**Excerpted from *Fifty Years in China*. 1910:217 - 218. Philadelphia: J. B. Lippincott Company.**

New Words and Expressions

identical [ɑiˈdentik(ə)l]adj. 同一的;完全相同的 n. 完全相同的事物

pictorial [pikˈtɔːriəl]adj. 绘画的;形象化的 n. 画报;画刊

patron [ˈpetrən]n. 赞助人;保护人;主顾

guild [gild]n. 协会;行会;同业公会

render [ˈrendə]vt. 致使;提出;实施;着色;以……回报 vi. 给予补偿 n. 打底;交纳;粉刷

expatiate [ikˈspeiʃieit]vi. 详述;细说;漫游

derive [diˈraiv]vt. 源于;得自;获得 vi. 起源

bulk [bʌlk]n. 体积;容量;大多数;大块 vt. 使扩大;使形成大量;使显得重要

stroll [strəul]n. 漫步;巡回演出 vt. 散步;闲逛 vi. 散步;闲逛;巡回演出

subscription [səbˈskripʃən]n. 捐献;订阅;订金;签署

Notes

1. There, as now in China, we see a stage composed of a square platform projecting into the pit, with a door of entrance and a door of exit on each side of the rear wall(paragraph 1):这里用到 see sth/sb doing sth，表示看到的动作或状态正在进行。

如:She was seen running away from the scene of the crime.

有人看见她从犯罪现场跑开。

此外，本句中 project into 意为"投射;投入…… 中"。

如:A missile was projected into space.

导弹被发射升空。

2. It is particularly noticeable that the pit, in all theatrical representations in China, whether given in the courtyards of the temples, in the halls of the guilds (paragraph 1)：这里的“in all theatrical representations in China, whether given in the courtyards of the temples, in the halls of the guilds”用作插入语，是对本句话的一些附加解释、说明或总结。

三、思考题

1. 如何理解立德在中国描写中“一方面极力赞扬中国古代文化，另一方面又以西方文化优越感的姿态抨击近代中国社会的落后”的二重心态？

2. 文中哪些方面可以看出立德在描写中国风土人情时体现出的深刻洞察力与感悟？

第七章

我的北京花园、亲密接触中国

一、作品导读

阿奇博尔德·立德夫人(Mrs. Archibald Little,1845—1926),原名阿丽霞·海伦·乃娃·毕维克(Alicia Helen Neva Bewicke),是英国商人、冒险家阿奇博尔德·约翰·立德(Archibald John Little,1838—1908)的妻子,因而她习惯被称为"立德夫人",国内有研究者或译者将她翻译为"阿奇博尔德·立德夫人"。

阿奇博尔德·立德夫人随丈夫在华生活时间长达20年(1887—1907),成为中国女权活动家和中国问题研究专家。1895年,立德夫人和其他九位在华女性成立"天足会",呼吁废除摧残女性的陋习。她通过在中国旅行、考察、社会活动等亲身经历,以阿奇博尔德·立德夫人(下文称"立德夫人")为名著文并发表有关中国题材的英文著作9部:The Fairy Foxes: *A Chinese Legend*(《狐仙:一个中国传奇》),Shanghai: Kelly &Walsh, 1890; *My Diary in A Chinese Farm*(《中国农村日记》),Shanghai: Kelly &Walsh, 1894; *A Marriage in China*(《中国婚事》),London: F. V. White, 1896; *Intimate China: the Chinese as I Have Seen Them*(《走近中国:我所见到的中国人》),London: Hutchinson & Co., 1899; *The Land of the Blue Gown*(《穿蓝色长袍的国度》),London: T. Fisher Unwin, 1901; *Out in China*(《在中国》), London: Trehere, 1902; *Li Hung Chang: His Life and Times*(《李鸿章:他的生活和时代》),London: Cassell&Co., 1903; *Guide to Peking*(《北京指南》),Tientsin: Tientsin Press, 1904; *Round about My Peking Garden*(《我的北京花园》),London: T. Fisher Unwin, 1905。

立德夫人作为晚清时期来华颇具代表性的亲历中国的旅行者，她著作中的游记作品非常受欢迎，她的来华游记讲述了作为一个外国人十多年来在中国城市、乡村的所见所闻，细致地描绘了不同地方的风俗民情，深入地挖掘了中华民族的特性，她的游记中塑造的中国形象具有多重性。

《我的北京花园》记录的是立德夫人1900年至1902年间她在北京短暂居住以及在周边旅行时的见闻与感想，涉及历史、地理、宗教、教育、晚清官僚体制等多个方面，其间的时代背景较为复杂，八国联军入侵中国、慈禧太后挟光绪帝仓皇西逃后又还都、义和团遭镇压等事件导致神州大地动荡不安。立德夫人在书中不仅细致地描绘了北京以及周边地区的名胜古迹、自然风光和社会风俗，而且详尽地记录了当时社会背景下的生活场景与历史事件。书中立德夫人流露出对遭到战乱洗劫的中国古代文化痛惜之情，同时她也坚信中华民族的未来将发生巨大的变化。

《亲密接触中国》是立德夫人以一个晚清时期来华旅行者的身份与视角对晚清社会做了详尽描绘的作品，书中涉及的人物上至慈禧、光绪、清朝高官，下至士兵、普通百姓，雅致文人墨客，俗至市井无赖，涉及清末的中国城市、乡村、官场、科举、妇女缠足等社会的方方面面。纵观《亲密接触中国》一书，我们不难看出立德夫人对中国表现出的复杂情感：一方面赞扬中国人人性中的中和善良之美，同情中国落后及其中国人的艰难处境；另一方面西方文化中心论和优越感占据着她的头脑，导致她存在着希望中国皈依基督教、受控于英国的幻想。

二、作品选读

1.《我的北京花园》

Episode Ⅰ

And so far it has been contrived that every house shall have its own seaview. Then when one goes to the East Cliff the extraordinary beauty of the still, vast, dreamlike view spread out before the eye is almost overwhelming in its haunting loveliness. One might compare it with that from the Waldron Hill at Torquay, but lovely as that is, it is a pigmy by comparison. To look over the Bay of Naples must always be a rare pleasure, but this view which is as much larger as China is larger than Italy. It is its sublimity that at once strikes the beholder dumb, next the exquisite, as it would seem, never-ending variety of shades of blue. Only very gradually one appreciates its infinite variety of detail. There are the beautiful mountains behind Shan-hai-kwan merged in yet higher ranges, now become apparent, and continuing a long and ever-varying barrier range past Pei-tai-ho on and on into the west. I forget how many watch towers scattered along the Great Wall a gentleman told me he could count from there, but I know it ran into the thirties. The day we saw it first there was a slight blue haze, making everything perhaps more lovely, but obscuring details, yet we got tired of counting towers, following with our eyes the gallant leaps and courtesies of that Great Wall, which becomes a sort of culte as one stays on in its sphere of influence. Although, of course, in the more frequented, more necessary parts, it must have been often repaired since then, it is so marvelous to think of its having been built over two thousand years ago—the ten thousand li wall, as the Chinese call it, that is at least three thousand miles, and, as is said, in ten years, and so well built too—that portions of it should still survive! How many people there must have been even in those days! How well they must have been organized! How much under control.

...

I feel I have not done justice to Pei-tai-ho. Nowhere in Europe have I seen a seaside resort such an agreeable mixture of country and seaside. Everyday one stays there one becomes aware of fresh beauties in it, new and entrancing view-points. It may not in itself be very much to look at from a distance, but there could not be a more delightful place to look out from. There are hills close at hand for walks. Whilst the beauty of various spots on the mountains forming its background, and to be reached in a day's journey, must surely be such as it would be very hard to beat anywhere for grandeur.

——**Excerpted from *Around About My Peking Garden*. 1905: 119 – 122. London: T. Fisher Unwin.**

New Words and Expressions

contrive [kən'traiv]vt. 设计；发明；图谋 vi. 谋划；设法做到

haunting ['hɔːntiŋ]adj. 不易忘怀的；萦绕于心头的

pigmy ['pigmi]n. 矮人；侏儒；微不足道的东西/人 adj. 矮小的；无足轻重的

sublimity [sə'blimiti]n. 崇高；庄严；气质高尚

exquisite ['ekskwizit]adj. 精致的；细腻的；优美的；高雅的

haze [heiz]n. 阴霾；薄雾；疑惑 vt. 使变朦胧；使变糊涂 vi. 变朦胧；变糊涂

obscure [əb'skjʊr]n. 模糊 v. 使……含糊；隐藏

courtesy ['kɜːtisi]n. 礼貌；好意；恩惠 adj. 殷勤的；出于礼节的

sphere [sfiə]n. 范围；球体 vt. 包围；放入球内 adj. 球体的

entrancing [in'trænsiŋ]adj. 使人入神的；令人欣喜的

grandeur ['grændjə]n. 壮丽；庄严；宏伟

Notes

1. One might compare it with that from the Waldron Hill at Torquay, but lovely as that is, it is a pigmy by comparison(paragraph 1)：此句中的"but lovely as that is"是由 as 引导的让步状语从句，意为"尽管；虽然"，常可将作表语或作状语的形容词、名词、副词以及情态动词或助动词之后的动词原形提到句首，构成倒装形式。

如：(1) Tired as he is, he offers to help me.

尽管他已经很累了，他还是主动提出帮助我。

(2) Well-written as the book is, the author is not satisfied and

prepared to revise it.

尽管这本书写得很好，作者还是不满意并打算修改它。

(3) Student as he is, he does not study hard.

他虽然是个学生，却不努力学习。(注:做表语的名词提前时不能用冠词)

(4) Much as I admire his courage, I don't think he acted wisely.

我虽然崇拜他的勇气，但我认为他这样做是不明智的。

(5) Try as you will, you won't be able to persuade him.

不管你怎么努力，你都说服不了他。

2. To look over the Bay of Naples must always be a rare pleasure, but this view is as much larger as China is larger than Italy(paragraph 1):第一个 as 作副词，表示程度，意为“同样地”;第二个 as 作连词，表示“正如;正像;像”等。“as China is larger than Italy”意为“正如中国比意大利更大一样。”

3. It must have been often repaired since then, it is so marvelous to think of its having been built over two thousand years ago(paragraph 1):此句中用到了情态动词的完成时态，must have been 表示对过去已经发生的事情的肯定推测。

如: He must have gone to bed, for the light was out.

其他类似的用法有:can/could/may/might/can't/should have done

如:(1) You could have done it better.

你本可以把这件事做得更好。

(2) He might have gone to the library.

他或许已经去图书馆了。

(3) You should have been more careful in driving your car.

开车时你本应该更加小心些。

(4) Mike can't have found his car, for he came to work by bus this morning.

迈克不可能找到他的车，因为他早上是坐公交去上班。

4. I feel I have not done justice to Pei-tai-ho. Nowhere in Europe have I seen a seaside resort such an agreeable mixture of country and seaside (paragraph 2):此句中的 do justice 意为“ 公平地对待;说句公道话”。

如:(1) We should do justice to everyone.

我们应该公正地对待每个人。

(2) To do him justice, he has done something valuable for the Chinese revolution.

公平地说，他为中国革命做过一些有价值的工作。

Episode Ⅱ

We may in any case look for a great change in China in the course of the next few years. The Chinese are seeking instruction in modern science, and all through the length and breadth of China Japanese instructors are to be found. Thus even Peking may be different before we again revisit it, and these pages tell to future travelers rather what used to be seen there than what they are likely to discover. This volume is but a little tribute to a time of dalliance in one of China's many pleasant places. Since then I have dwelt in a Yunnan garden, and the Yunnan garden, by the freshness of its air and its beautiful cloud effects, has somewhat dimmed the recollection of Peking with its dust clouds and its old world grandeur. But Peking, Constantinople, Athens, Rome must for ever remain special places in the history of the world. Shall we someday add to them our own capital of London? Already there are so many ominous signs of the handwriting upon the wall. And as Chinese say—"If Fortune smiles—who doesn't? If Fortune doesn't, who does?" When a city once begins to change from being a mighty factor in the present to a grand relic of the past, the degeneration always goes forward with geometrical rather than arithmetical rapidity. Peking would not have believed under its first Manchu rulers that it could ever be possible for it to stand passive by whilst Russians and Japanese fought for the first place in its direction, across and around the very birthplace of the dynasty.

Then it became, as Li Hung Chang once said of it, a museum. "Having visited all Europe", he said, "I have seen the museums in all your capitals. Peking had its museum also, for the whole Imperial city was a museum, begun centuries ago, which one might compare with the most beautiful of yours—and now it is in ruins!" But it may yet be built up again and begin a new order of things. Who can forecast the future? It is far easier to string together broken recollections of the Past.

Yet it is but by a study of the Past, together with a careful consideration of human character, that we can form any idea of what the Future may have in store, or, which is the matter of real practical importance, of what is the line of action it is discreet for us ourselves, either as a nation or as individuals, to pursue. For the party leader the signs of the times may suffice, but the far-seeing statesman moulds the Future by his handling of the Present based upon consideration of the Past.

Peking's whole history may be viewed as a demonstration of the futility of Opportunism in dealing with the destinies of one of the greatest nations the world has yet seen. Yet for some centuries of extraordinary brilliance who could have believed it would prove a failure? The whole Chinese nation knows it now, harassed by the sense that, instead of proving a frontier fortress, a bulwark against invasion, a capital on the borders of an unwieldy empire may at any time be used as a menace by an adroit enemy, and thus impart a sense of insecurity to the whole body politic.

That the Peking Government has also for many years now been out of touch with the rest of the nation, but no one can doubt who knows China. Yet it was a great conception and beautiful even in its decay.

——**Excerpted from *Around About My Peking Garden*. 1905: 277 - 279. London: T. Fisher Unwin.**

New Words and Expressions

tribute ['tribju:t]n. 礼物;颂词;悼念;吊唁礼物

dalliance ['dæliəns]n. 嬉戏;闲混;调情

dwelt [dwelt]v. 居住;老是想着(dwell 的过去分词)

dim [dim]adj. 暗淡的;昏暗的;怀疑的 vt. 使暗淡;使变模糊 vi. 变模糊

ominous ['ɒminəs]adj. 预兆的;不吉利的

relic ['relik]n. 遗迹;遗物;废墟;纪念物

degeneration [di, dʒenə'reiʃ(ə)n]n. 退化;[医] 变性;堕落;恶化

geometrical [dʒiə'metrikl]adj. 几何的;几何学的

arithmetical [æriθ'mεtikl]adj. 算术的;算术上的

discreet [di'skriːt]adj. 谨慎的;小心的

suffice [sə'fais]vt. 使满足;足够……用;合格 vi. 足够;有能力

mould [məʊld]vi. 发霉 vt. 浇铸;用泥土覆盖 n. 模具;霉

futility [fjuː'tiliti]n. 无用;徒劳;无价值

opportunism [ɑpə'tunizəm]n. 机会主义;投机主义

harass ['hærəs;hə'ræs]vt. 使困扰;使烦恼;反复袭击

bulwark ['bʊlwək]n. 壁垒;保障;防波堤 vt. 保护;筑垒保卫

unwieldy [ʌn'wiːldi]adj. 笨拙的;笨重的;不灵便的;难处理的

menace ['menəs]n. 威胁;恐吓 vi. &vt. 恐吓;威胁

adroit [ə'drɒit]adj. 敏捷的;灵巧的;熟练的

politic ['pɒlitik]adj. 精明的;有策略的;狡猾的;审慎的 vi. 拉选票

Notes

1. Thus even Peking may be different before we again revisit it, and these pages tell to future travelers rather what used to be seen there than what they are likely to discover(paragraph 1):此句中 rather...than 结构意为"是……而不是……",连接前后两个并列成分。

如:I would rather watch TV at home than go to the cinema.

我宁可在家看电视而不愿去看电影。

2. This volume is but a little tribute to a time of dalliance in one of China's many pleasant places(paragraph 1):此句中的 but 用作副词,意思上相当于 only,后面跟名词或动词。

如:(1) Tom is but a child. 汤姆只是个孩子。

(2)We can but try now. 我们现在只有尝试一遍。

3. It is far easier to string together broken recollections of the Past (paragraph 2):此句中的 far 用作副词,表示程度,修饰其后的形容词或副词的比较级,与此类似的副词还有 much, still, even, a little, a bit,

rather, far, by far, a lot, a great deal 等。

如:(1) He is no richer than Peter.

他不比彼得富裕多。

(2)Matters are a lot better than ever before.

情况远远比以往好。

(3)The room is a bit larger than that one.

这个房间比那个稍大一点。

(4)He works still harder than ever.

他比以往更加努力学习了。

4. Yet it is but by a study of the Past, together with a careful consideration of human character, that we can form any idea of what the Future may have in store, or, which is the matter of real practical importance, of what is the line of action it is discreet for us ourselves, either as a nation or as individuals, to pursue(paragraph 3):此句中是由 it is...that... 引导的强调句,用来强调方式状语"by a study of the Past, together with a careful consideration of human character"。

在英语中,通常可以用 it is/ was +that/ who 的结构来表示强调,强调句型是通过 it 强调词来改变句子结构,使句子的某一成分受到强调而构成的强调结构,基本句型是:It is/ was + 被强调部分(通常是主语、宾语或状语)+ that/ who(当强调主语且主语指人)+ 其他部分。强调句可以强调除谓语以外的一切成分。

如针对"I met Li Ming at the railway station yesterday". 这一句子进行强调。

强调主语:It was I that (who) met Li Ming at the railway station yesterday.

强调宾语:It was Li Ming that I met at the railway station yesterday.

强调地点状语:It was at the railway station that I met Li Ming yesterday.

强调时间状语:It was yesterday that I met Li Ming at the railway station.

2.《亲密接触中国》

Episode Ⅰ

It was in the merry month of May, 1887, that I first landed in China; but from the first there was nothing merry about China. It felt bitterly cold, after passing through the tropics; and in Shanghai one shivered in a warm wrap, as the wind blew direct from the North Pole straight at one's chest, till one day it suddenly turned quite hot, and all clothes felt too heavy. Every one almost knows what Shanghai is like. It has been admirably described over and over again, with its rows of fine European houses fronting the river, the beautiful public gardens and well-trodden grass-plats interposed between the two; with its electric lights and its carriages, and great European stores, at which you can buy everything you could possibly want only a very little dearer than in London. There used to be nothing romantic or Eastern about it. Now, darkened by the smoke of over thirty factories, it is flooded by an ever-increasing Chinese population, who jostle with Europeans in the thoroughfare, till it seems as if the struggle between the two races would be settled in the streets of Shanghai, and the European get driven to the wall. For the Chinaman always goes a steady pace, and in his many garments, one upon the top of the other, presents a solid, impenetrable front to the hurrying European; whilst the wheelbarrows on which his womankind are conveyed rush in and out amongst the carriages, colliding here and there with a coolie-drawn rickshaw, and always threatening the toes of the foot-passenger. Too often there are no foot-pavements, and the whole motley crowd at its very varying paces is forced on to the muddy street. Ever and anon even now a closed sedan-chair, with some wealthy Chinaman from the adjacent Chinese city, threads its way in and out among the vehicles, noiseless and stealthy, a reminder of China's past glories. There are also now wholly Chinese streets in the foreign settlement, where all the shop-fronts are gorgeous with gilding and fine decorative Chinese characters, where all the shops have signs which hang perpendicularly across the street- way, instead of horizontally over the shop-front as with us, and where Chinese shop keepers sit inside, bare to the waist, in summer presenting a most unpleasing picture of too much flesh, and in winter masses of fur and satin.

Shanghai has got a capital racecourse, and theatre, and cricket-ground—grounds for every kind of sport, indeed. It has a first-rate club, and an ill-kept museum. Its sights are the bubbling well and the tea-garden in the China town, believed by globe-trotters, but erroneously, to be the original of the willow-pattern plate. Beside this, there is what is called the Stone Garden, full of picturesque bits. A great deal that is interesting is to be seen in the China town by those who can detach their minds from the dirt; in one part all the houses have drawbridges leading to them. But even the Soochow Road in the foreign settlement has never yet been treated pictorially as it deserves. It is the Palais Royal of "Chinese Shanghai". At the hour when carriage traffic may only pass one way because of the crowd, it would reward an Alma-Tadema to depict the Chinese dandies filling all its many balconies, pale and silken clad, craning their necks to see, and by the haughtiness of their gaze recalling the decadent Romans of the last days of the empire. Their silken garments, their arched mouths, the coldness of their icy stare, has not yet been duly depicted. *Chun Ti Kung*, by the late Mr. Claude Rees, is so far the only attempt to describe their life. Yet they, too, have souls possibly worth the awakening. With their long nails, their musk-scented garments, their ivory opium-pipes, and delicate arrangements of colors, they cannot be without sensibilities. Do they feel that the Gaul is at the gates, and that the China of their childhood is passing away ?

…

But here let me record my first great disappointment, because it may be that of many another. Brown mud is the first thing one sees of China. Brown mud accompanies the traveler for miles along the Yangtze River, all along the Peiho, up to brown and muddy Tientsin, and on up to Peking itself. China generally is not at all like the willow-pattern plate. I do not know if I really had expected it to be blue and white ; but it was a disappointment to find it so very brown and muddy.

——Excerpted from *Intimate China*. 1899: 1 – 4. London: Hutchinson & Co.

New Words and Expressions

tropics ['trɒpiks]n. 热带地区

shiver ['ʃivə]n. 颤抖;战栗;碎片 vi. 颤抖;哆嗦;打碎 vt. 颤抖;打碎

wrap [ræp]vt. 包;缠绕;隐藏;掩护 vi. 包起来;缠绕 n. 外套;围巾

well-trodden ['wel'trɔdən]adj. 常到的;陈腐的;用旧了的

interpose [intə'pəʊz]vt. 提出(异议等);使插入;使干涉 vi. 干预;插入;调停

jostle ['dʒɒs(ə)l]n. 推撞;拥挤 vi. 竞争;争夺;推挤 vt. 推挤;撞;争夺

thoroughfare ['θʌrəfeə]n. 大道;通路

garment ['gɑːm(ə)nt]n. 衣服;服装;外表;外观 vt. 给……穿衣服

impenetrable [im'penitrəb(ə)l]adj. 不能通过的;顽固的;费解的;不接纳的

whilst [wɑilst]conj. 同时;时时;有时;当……的时候

wheelbarrow ['wiːlbærəʊ]n. 独轮手推车 vt. 用于推车运送

womankind ['wʊmənkɑind]n. 女性;妇女们

coolie ['kuːli]n. (印度的)苦力;小工

rickshaw ['rikʃɔː]n. (等于 ricksha)人力车;黄包车

pavement ['peivm(ə)nt]n. 人行道;路面

motley ['mɒtli]adj. 杂色的;混杂的 n. 混杂;杂色衣服;小丑

anon [ə'nɒn]adv. 不久;立刻;另一次

adjacent [ə'dʒeis(ə)nt]adj. 邻近的;毗连的

thread [θred]n. 线;螺纹;思路;衣服 vi. &vt. 穿过;穿线于;交织

stealthy ['stelθi]adj. 鬼鬼祟祟的;秘密的

gilding ['gildiŋ]n. 镀金;虚饰的外观 v. 镀金;虚饰(gild 的现在分词)

decorative [ˈdek(ə)rətiv]adj. 装饰性的；装潢用的

perpendicularly [pəːpənˈdikjuləli]adv. 垂直地；直立地

horizontally [hɑrəˈzɑntli]adv. 水平地；地平地

satin [ˈsætin]n. 缎子；缎子衣服 adj. 光滑的；绸缎做的；似缎的

racecourse [ˈreiskɔːs]n. 赛马场；跑马场；跑道

bubble [ˈbʌb(ə)l]n. 气泡；泡沫；泡状物 vi. &vt. 沸腾；冒泡；滔滔不绝地说

globe-trotter n. 周游世界者

erroneously [iˈrəuniəsli]adv. 错误地；不正确地

willow-pattern plate 青花瓷盘

picturesque [piktʃəˈresk]adj. 独特的；生动的；别致的；图画般的

detach [diˈtætʃ]vt. 分离；派遣；使超然

drawbridge [ˈdrɔːbridʒ]n. (可开闭的)吊桥

pictorially [pikˈtɔriəli]adv. 绘画般地

depict [diˈpikt]vt. 描述；描画

dandy [ˈdændi]adj. 上等的；极好的；服装华丽的 n. 花花公子；好打扮的人

clad [klæd]adj. 穿衣的；覆盖的

crane [krein]n. 吊车；起重机；鹤 vi. 伸着脖子看；迟疑；踌躇

haughtiness [ˈhɔːtinis]n. 傲慢；不逊

decadent [ˈdekəd(ə)nt]adj. 颓废的；衰微的 n. 颓废者

musk [mʌsk]n. 麝香；麝香鹿；麝香香味

opium [ˈəʊpiəm]n. 鸦片；麻醉剂 adj. 鸦片的

Notes

1. There used to be nothing romantic or Eastern about it(paragraph 1): used to 表示过去经常的习惯，但现在不再这样了，常译为“过去常常”。其中的 to 是不定式符号，后面要接动词原形。它只有过去式一种形式，可以用于所有人称。

如：(1) I used to watch TV, but now I don't like it.

我过去常常看电视，但现在不喜欢了。

(2)He used to like collecting coins.

他过去喜欢集硬币。

2. Now, darkened by the smoke of over thirty factories, it is flooded by an ever-increasing Chinese population, who jostle with Europeans in the thoroughfare, till it seems as if the struggle between the two races would be settled in the streets of Shanghai, and the European get driven to the wall(paragraph 1):此句中的 darkened by the smoke of over thirty factories 属于过去分词短语，在此做伴随状语。过去分词短语作状语时，表示被动的或已完成的动作，在句中可作时间、原因、条件、让步、方式、伴随状语等。

如:(1)Much discouraged, she moved on to London.

她很沮丧，搬到了伦敦。(用作原因状语)

(2)Compared with you, I still have a long way to go.

跟你比较起来，我还差得很远呢。(用作条件状语)

(3)He came in, followed by his wife.

他走了进来，后面跟着他的妻子。(用作伴随状语)

(4)He died, leaving his wife with five children.

他死了，留下他妻子和五个孩子。(用作结果状语)

3. There are also now wholly Chinese streets in the foreign settlement, where all the shop-fronts are gorgeous with gilding and fine decorative Chinese characters, where all the shops have signs which hang perpendicularly across the street- way, instead of horizontally over the shop-front as with us, and where Chinese shop keepers sit inside, bare to the waist, in summer presenting a most unpleasing picture of too much flesh, and in winter masses of fur and satin(paragraph 2):先行词表示地点的，并在定语从句中做状语的(不做主语、表语和宾语)，用 where 引导定语从句。

如:(1) This is the house where I once lived.

这是我曾经住过的房子。

(2)You reach a point where medicine can't help.

你已到了药物无法治疗的地步。

(3)It's put me in a position where I can't afford to take the job.

这使我陷入一种不能接受此工作的境地。

Episode Ⅱ

There are many summer trips that are a joy in the remembering, but a trip to Chinese Tibet had never fallen to the lot of any European woman before. And it was the more delightful, perhaps, because we never thought of anything of the kind when we started. But there is a drawback to living on a mountain-summit that it is such a climb to come back again when you go out; and our quarters on Mount Omi were not too comfortable! Only one small room for living and sleeping in, like a back room in a Canadian log hut, and without a window to open, makes one restless after a time. So we thought we would gently stroll on to another sacred mountain, whose flat top was a very striking feature in the landscape. And we went down into what is called the Wilderness, where there are wild cattle and wild men, and for about a week wandered on, passing along by the boundary of the unconquered Lolos, and up the most magnificent ravine. I have seen or can imagine, down which a torrent had swept but a week before from the Sai King, or Drying Prayerbooks Mountain, to which we were bound, drowning twenty-six people in one hamlet alone.

Climbing the Sai King was rather a formidable affair. But for the guidance of a young priest, returning from one of those begging excursions by means of which he had bought the whole mountain-summit, we never should have reached the top before darkness set in; and in the dark no man would dare to move upon the Sai King. For not only are there all manner of wild beasts, but the path leads along the narrow edge of a col, and then up staircases, till at last you arrive at three ladders, one of twenty-seven rungs, before you find yourself at the top of the awful precipices that girdle it all round, in a sort of park with firs and rhododendrons, the latter at least twenty feet high, moss hanging from them in garlands, as well as a foot deep upon the ground. It is a veritable boys' paradise (and as such I have described it at length in the *Nineteenth Century* of January, 1896), with squirrels and deer and birds innumerable, large very sweet white strawberries in the greatest profusion, raspberries abundant, currants plentiful, mushrooms in bushels. There are glorious views from the brink of precipices, when you can break your way through the rhododendrons and look over, hearing the rivers murmuring some five or six thousand feet below, and seeing the Tibetan summits like a sea of mountains.

——**Excerpted from *Intimate China*. 1899: 396 – 398. London: Hutchinson & Co.**

Words and expressions

quarter ['kwɔːtə]n. 四分之一;地区;季度 vi. 住宿;驻扎 vt. 将……四等分

sacred ['seikrid]adj. 神的;神圣的;宗教的;庄严的

ravine [rə'viːn]n. 沟壑;山涧;峡谷

torrent ['tɒr(ə)nt]n. 奔流;倾注;迸发;连续不断

hamlet ['hæmlit]n. 小村庄

formidable ['fɔːmidəb(ə)l]adj. 强大的;可怕的;令人敬畏的;艰难的

excursion [ik'skɜːʃ(ə)n]n. 偏移;远足;短程旅行;离题;游览,游览团

rung [rʌŋ]n. 横档;脚蹬横木;地位

precipice ['presipis]n. 悬崖;绝壁;险境

girdle ['gɜːd(ə)l]n. 腰带;围绕物 vt. 围绕;绕……而行;用带子捆扎

rhododendron [,rəʊdə'dendr(ə)n]n. 杜鹃花

garland ['gɑːlənd]n. 花环 vt. 戴花环

veritable ['veritəb(ə)l]adj. 真正的;名副其实的

squirrel ['skwir(ə)l]n. 松鼠;松鼠毛皮 vt. 贮藏

innumerable [i'njuːm(ə)rəb(ə)l]adj. 无数的;数不清的

profusion [prə'fjuːʒ(ə)n]n. 丰富;充沛;慷慨

raspberry ['rɑːzb(ə)ri]n. 覆盆子

currant ['kʌr(ə)nt]n. 红醋栗;无籽葡萄干;红醋药

brink [briŋk]n. (峭壁的)边缘

Notes

1. But there is a drawback to living on a mountain-summit that it is such a climb to come back again when you go out(paragraph 1):此句中的 there is a drawback to 的"to"是介词，其后接名词或者动名词。

2. We never should have reached the top before darkness set in (paragraph 2):本句用到了情态动词的完成时态:should have said 是情态动词 should+have+done 的结构，表示"应该做而未做"，本身是表示否定的意义，但前面又有一个否定 never，所以是双重否定表肯定，意思是"我本不该"。

三、思考题

1. 立德夫人的游记中塑造中国形象的多重性体现在哪些方面?
2. 结合节选文本，如何理解立德夫人在描绘中国时体现的双重心态?

第八章

亲历晚清四十五年

一、作品导读

李提摩太(Timothy Richard,1845—1919),出生于英国威尔士卡马孙郡,英国浸礼会传教士。1870 年,李提摩太受英浸礼会派遣来到中国,开始在山东、东北一带传教,同时学习佛教、儒家和伊斯兰教著作。1876 年,山东发生规模较大的旱灾,李提摩太为灾民募集救灾物款。1878 年,山西发生严重灾荒,李提摩太去山西赈济灾民,并在山西太原开始传教。除了传教,他担任过天津《时报》主笔,担任过同文书会督办(他将同文书会改为“广学会”),他主持广学会 25 年期间,出版了《万国公报》等十几种报刊、2000 种书籍和小册子,成为当时中国规模较大的出版机构之一。同时,李提摩太也是山西大学堂西学专斋(今山西大学)的创始人之一。可以说,李提摩太在宗教、科学、通讯、国际贸易、赈灾、现代学校和专业学院的创设、现代出版社的建立等多个领域参与了中国历史的进程,他不仅是一位有影响的宗教人士,同时也是中外达官贵人的座上宾。他一生著述颇丰,主要有《亲历晚清四十五年》《七国新学备要》《天下五大洲各大国》《百年一觉》《欧洲八大帝王传》《泰西新史揽要》等 20 多种。

《亲历晚清四十五年》一书详细记录了作者在中国长达 45 年传教的经历,在传教的同时,他“结交权贵,联络士绅,顾问洋务,鼓吹变法,调停外交,抨击革命,时而幕后,时而台前,不辞劳苦,忙忙碌碌奔走于红尘深处,在不同政治势力之间纵横捭阖,成为清末大变局中的一位风云人物,在中国近代史上留下了不可磨灭的印记。”《亲历晚清四十五年》中所写旅行游记真实、深刻,不乏生动之处,这对我们了解当时在中国旅行情况具有重要的参考价值,如书中第十三章《天台山之行》的“旅行者的代理机构”一节,就写到 100

多年前杭州旅游就有统一套票出售了。

纵观《亲历晚清四十五年》一书，我们可以客观公正地评价李提摩太。一方面他大量引进、传播西方科技文化知识和社会治理之道，对当时中国开启民智和推动社会变革方面做出了不可抹杀的贡献；另一方面他的人生立场、价值取向都受历史时代限制，他不自觉地充当了历史意志的工具和殖民时代的代言人，成为西方强势文明对外扩张的先锋和代表人物。

以下节选的是李提摩太在中国西北部、山西和浙江的旅行见闻。

二、作品选读

Episode Ⅰ

The roads in China are most extraordinary. The plains of Shantung, Chihli, and Honan are composed of yellow soil brought down by the Yellow River; in Shansi there are strange formations of loess in which the country people dig cave dwellings, delightfully cool in summer, and warm in winter. As the climate is very dry in these provinces, sometimes without a drop of rain for six months, the carts travel with ease along the dusty roads, for not a stone is to be seen for a hundred miles. But when the rainy season comes in June, July and August, the roads are drowned with water, which when mixed with the dust forms impassable sloughs of mud. All traffic ceases along these highways, and for three months there used to be a stoppage of trade, all capital being locked up during this time without any interest, involving enormous loss to China as a whole.

A similar stoppage of trade arose from the narrowness of the streets in larger cities. In Tientsin the streets were not wide enough to allow two carts to pass each other. This always involved great wrangling between the carters as to which should back his cart to the end of the street. Sometimes other carts came behind the first one, and there would be a block of some dozen or more carts, involving a delay of hours. The time wasted involved so much loss to the merchants that it would have paid them to buy up a portion of the city and lay it out with wide streets. What sober officials and business men did not attempt, the Boxers did in one day. They burned the city down. In rebuilding the authorities laid out streets wide enough for carts and tramcars to pass, to the great gain of all.

In those days in North China officials used to travel in sedan-chairs, carried according to rank by four or eight bearers, at the rate of about twenty miles a day. Another mode of travel was the lighter shen-tze, an erection covered with matting and slung between two mules, one in front and one behind. Merchants as a rule travelled in a small covered cart at the rate of about thirty miles a day. They started on the day's journey about an hour before dawn, and travelled till about ten, when the carters stopped to feed the mules and have a midday meal. About noon they started again, and travelled till a little before dark, when they put up at an inn lest they should be attacked by robbers. There were, and are, regular inns on the great highways.

At the best inns all kinds of food can be procured, and excellently cooked chicken, fish, pork, and eggs, prepared in many different ways. The dish of fried pork and cabbage is as common as ham and eggs in England. The available vegetables comprise potatoes, sweet potatoes, yams, cabbages, turnips, carrots, egg plants, beans, peas, plums, cucumber, while fruit of various kinds—cherries, pears, plums, peaches, apples, apricots, persimmons, melons, grapes—can be obtained at different seasons of the year, with nuts of different kinds—peanuts, chestnuts, water-chestnuts, and lotus seeds. Alcohol made of the tall millet, a sherry-like yellow wine, rice wine, and wine made from small millet can be served, and is always drunk hot. The rule is to take the table fare provided for all alike. The muleteers have the same food as their masters, but sit at a different table. The noon meal usually costs two hundred cash, the evening meal about three hundred cash, which includes the night's lodging, and ten percent, is paid in tips to the waiters.

Altogether the noonday meal costs about six pence and the evening meal about nine pence.

Besides the above quick mode of travelling in North China, there is the much slower but commoner one of the barrow. This vehicle is peculiar to China, and unlike any in Europe or America. In the centre is a stout wheel, about three feet high, as strong as a cartwheel. On it is fixed a framework, carrying a seat on each side of the wheel. The traveler sits on one side, while his goods balance him on the other. The barrow is pushed from behind by a coolie, and pulled in front by another coolie or by a mule or donkey. The load which these barrows carry is enormous, sometimes half a ton, involving an enormous strain on the man pushing it. The converging shafts are so arranged that the greatest strain is thrown on the wheel. These barrows travel at the rate of about twenty miles a day. The inns at which they stay are much inferior in accommodation to those frequented by carters and muleteers. The k'ang is often only a foot high from the ground, and therefore damp, while the food is coarse, consisting of millet and maize, with salted vegetables, but no meat. In summer the barrow is covered with a blue awning, and one can read or lie down and sleep while the mile pulls the barrow along at a good pace. In Shantung it is a common sight to see sails fitted to the barrows when there is a good breeze. The sails of a dozen of these heavy-laden barrows travelling along a deep-cut road have the appearance of a fleet of boats scudding along before the wind down some unseen creek in the country. I once travelled with these slow barrowmen near the coast of Shantung, where the ground was white with deposits of soda exuding everywhere. I was warned of the difficulty of getting fresh water, as every well was saturated with soda. When we attempted to make tea, the soda in the water made the infusion very strong and bitter. Happily, I found a good remedy. I provided myself with a bagful of cucumbers, and when I suffered from thirst after the bitter tea the cucumbers tasted as sweet as apples.

——Excerpted from *Forty-Five Years in China*. 1916:73 – 75. London: T. Fisher Unwin LTD.

New Words and Expressions

cart [kɑ:t]n. 购物车；[车辆] 手推车

impassable [im'pɑ:səb(ə)l]adj. 不能通行的；无路可通的

slough [slɑʊ]n. 蜕下的皮(或壳)；绝境；vi. 蜕皮；脱落

stoppage ['stɒpidʒ]n. 停止；故障；罢工；堵塞；扣留

wrangle ['ræŋgl]n. 争论；吵嘴 vi. &vt. 争论；争吵

Boxers 义和团

tramcar ['træmkɑ:]n. (有轨)电车；矿车

sedan-chair [si'dæn- tʃeə]n. 轿子

erection [i'rekʃ(ə)n]n. 勃起；建造；建筑物；直立

matting ['mætiŋ]n. 席子 v. 铺席于……上；使……无光泽(mat 的-ing 形式)

slung [slʌŋ]v. 投掷；悬挂(sling 的过去分词)

procure [prə'kjʊə]vt. 获得；取得；导致 vi. 取得

plum [plʌm]n. 李子；梅子 adj. 有利的；上等的

apricot ['eiprikɒt]n. 杏；杏子 adj. 杏黄色的

persimmon [pə'simən]n. 柿子；柿子树

melon ['melən]n. 瓜；甜瓜；大肚子

water-chestnut [wɔ:tə 'tʃesnʌt]n. 荸荠；菱角

millet ['milit]n. 小米；粟；稷；黍的籽实

sherry ['ʃɛri]n. 雪利酒(西班牙产的一种烈性白葡萄酒)；葡萄酒

muleteer [mju:li'tiə]n. 赶骡的人

barrow ['bærəʊ]n. 搬运架；手推车；弃矿；古坟

stout [stɑʊt]adj. 结实的；矮胖的；勇敢的 n. 矮胖子；烈性啤酒

coolie ['ku:li]n. (印度的)苦力；小工

converge [kən'vɜ:dʒ]vt. 使汇聚 vi. 聚集；靠拢；收敛

shaft [ʃɑ:ft]n. 拍杆；杆状物 vt. 利用；在……上装杆

coarse [kɔ:s]adj. 粗糙的；粗俗的；下等的

maize [meiz]adj. 黄色的；玉米色的 n. 玉米；黄色；玉米色

awning ['ɔ:niŋ]n. 雨篷；遮阳篷

scud [skʌd]n. 飞毛腿;疾行 vi. 疾行;顺风行驶

creek [kriːk]n. 小溪;小湾

exude [igˈzjuːd]vt. & vi. 散发;流出;发散

saturate [ˈsætʃəreit]vt. 浸透;使湿透;使饱和 adj. 浸透的;饱和的

infusion [inˈfjuːʒ(ə)n]n. 灌输;浸泡;注入物;激励

Notes

1. ...for not a stone is to be seen for a hundred miles(paragraph 1):本句中的 to be seen 属于不定式的被动，在此表示"即将或将要发生的动作"。

如:(1) The building to be built will be a hospital.

即将建造的大楼是家医院。

(2) There's nothing to be done with them.

它们已经无可救药了。

2. All traffic ceases along these highways, and for three months there used to be a stoppage of trade, all capital being locked up during this time without any interest(paragraph 1):本句用到了 there be 句子结构。there was (were)只是单纯对过去情况的描述，对现在的情况并无任何暗示,过去有,现在也许没有，也许有，也许有更多。there used to be 则是过去曾经有，强调曾经，美景不再，如今已经没有了。

如:(1) There used to be a big lake near my house, but now it's small.

我家附近曾经有一个大湖，可它现在却很小了。

(2) There used to be a bus stop on that corner.

那个拐角上过去有个公共汽车站。

3. About noon they started again, and travelled till a little before dark, when they put up at an inn lest they should be attacked by robbers (paragraph 3):lest 是从属连词，意为"以免;唯恐",常用于引导目的状语从句表示否定，只用于书面语。lest 在表示"惊恐""忧虑"的动词后引导宾语从句，相当于 that。lest 所引导的从句中谓语动词要用虚拟式，即"(should ＋)动词原形"。

如:(1) We hurried back to school lest it should rain.

我们匆匆忙忙地赶回学校，生怕天会下雨。

(2) They spoke in whispers lest they should be heard.

他们低声说话，唯恐被别人听见。

(3) We talked in a low voice lest we should wake the baby up.

我们小声说话以免吵醒婴儿。

Episode Ⅱ

When we reached the mountains, it was difficult to travel in carts because of the roughness of the rocky path, so I rode a mule. It was the month of November. The weather was bitterly cold, and in going over a mountain pass one of my heels got frostbitten. In these mountainous districts the inns are built in caves dug out of the loess formation. In the summer these are exceedingly cool, as the sun's rays do not penetrate them; but in winter, on the other hand, these cave inns are very warm and when there was fire under the k'ang it was most comforting after a day's ride in the intense cold to reach one of them.

T'ai-yuan fu, the capital of Shansi, is situated at the north end of a plateau extending some one hundred miles from north to south; about thirty miles wide and about three thousand feet above sea-level. Ch'ing-chow fu in Shantung, which I had left, is only about two hundred feet above sea-level. The winter in Shansi therefore was far severer. Fortunately, the province has abundant coal, both anthracite and bituminous.

I arrived in T'ai-yuan fu with only a small sum of about two thousand taels in hand. I had secured a passport from Li Hung-chang, the Viceroy of Chihli, in case there should be opposition to my travelling so far into the interior. In the interval we began to see some terrible sights, dead bodies, torn by dogs and wolves, lying by the roadside. These dreadful sights, together with the terrible cold, such as they had not experienced before, quite unnerved my two companions. Seeing that their hearts had turned back to their homes, I gave them leave to go back to Shantung. On their return, however, the people were very angry with them for abandoning me. "To think that you, being Chinese, and accustomed to the climate of your country, should leave a foreigner, unused to it, to face all the cold and perils and privation alone! Shame on you! It is a disgrace!" they cried. The two men, for very shame after such a reception, determined to return to me in Shansi, and after many weeks' absence rejoined me in Tai-yuan fu.

In those days there were no Protestant missionaries living in the province, but there was a Roman Catholic Bishop and about a dozen priests throughout Shansi, carrying on work that had been at first commenced during the time of the Jesuit ascendance in Peking, more than two hundred years before.

——**Excerpted from *Forty -Five Years in China*. 1916: 126 - 127. London: T. Fisher Unwin LTD.**

New Words and Expressions

frostbitten ['frɒst, bitn]adj. 冻伤的;受霜害的 v. 使冻伤(frostbite 的过去分词)

loess ['ləʊis; lɜːs]n. 黄土

penetrate ['penitreit]vt. 渗透;穿透;洞察 vi. 渗透;刺入;看透

comforting ['kʌmfətiŋ]adj. 安慰的;令人欣慰的 v. 安慰(comfort 的-ing 形式)

situate ['sitʃʊeit]vt. 使位于;使处于 adj. 位于……的

plateau ['plætəʊ]n. 高原;稳定阶段;停滞时期 adj. 高原印第安人的

anthracite ['ænθrəsait]n. 无烟煤

bituminous [bi'tjuːminəs]adj. 沥青的;含沥青的

tael [teil]n. 两;银两

interval ['intəv(ə)l]n. 间隔;间距;幕间休息

unnerved ['ʌn'nəːvd]adj. 气馁的;烦恼不安的 v. 使焦躁(unnerve 的过去分词形式)

peril ['peril]n. 危险;冒险 vt. 危及;置……于险境

privation [prai'veiʃ(ə)n]n. 贫困;丧失;被剥夺了某物的状态

rejoin [riː'dʒɒin]vi. & vt. 答辩;回答;重新聚合

protestant [ˈprɒtistənt]adj. 新教的；新教徒的 n. 新教；新教徒

missionary [ˈmiʃ(ə)n(ə)ri]adj. 传教的；传教士的 n. 传教士

catholic [kæθəlik]adj. 天主教的；宽宏大量的 n. 天主教徒；罗马天主教

bishop [ˈbiʃəp]n. 主教

priest [priːst]n. 牧师；神父；教士 vt. 使成为神职人员；任命……为祭司

commence [kəˈmens]vt. 开始；着手 vi. 使……开始；使……得学位

ascendance [əˈsɛndəns]n. 优势；权势；支配地位

Episode Ⅲ

For the convenience of travelers there is a fine agency, by means of which they are passed on from place to place at a regular fixed rate, whether they travel by boat or are carried in chairs overland. This saves delay in looking for boats or chairs or coolies, and the trouble of bargaining for anything. The traveler buys a ticket for the whole journey, and is handed on at each station without a word of strife or a minute's delay. Each coolie is paid four hundred cash per day-about tenpence.

On the way between Shaohing and Chinghien we travelled up-stream in a boat rowed by three men. The river is both tidal and subject to floods from the rain which comes down from the mountains. On the Shaohing route the mountains are in the distance, three to six miles away, while the flat country is studded all over with busy towns, and crossed in all directions by canals of clear water. Here we are close to the mountains, with only about a quarter of a mile of cultivated land intervening.

——**Excerpted from *Forty-Five Years in China*. 1916: 274. London: T. Fisher Unwin LTD.**

New Words and Expressions

overland [ˈəʊvəlænd]adj. 陆上的 adv. 经由陆路 vt. 转地放牧

strife [straif]n. 冲突；争吵；不和

up-stream 逆流；在上游

row [rəʊ]n. 行；排；划船 vt. 划船；使……成排

tidal [ˈtaid(ə)l]adj. 潮汐的；潮的；定时涨落的

stud [stʌd]n. 种马；大头钉 vt. 散布；装饰 adj. 种马的

cultivate [ˈkʌltiveit]vt. 培养；陶冶；耕作

intervene [intəˈviːn]vi. 干涉；调停；插入

Notes

1. For the convenience of travelers there is a fine agency(paragraph 1)：此句中的 for the convenience of 意为"为了……的便利"。

如：(1) A new general store has been built for the convenience of the residents.

为便利居民，新建了一个百货商店。

(2) The shop assistants sell goods from door to door for the convenience of the masses.

售货员送货上门，便利群众。

2. The river is both tidal and subject to floods from the rain which comes down from the mountains(paragraph 2)：此句中的 be subject to 意为"使服从于；使隶属于；使经受；使经历"等意思。

如：(1) You should subject yourself to my command.

你必须听从我的命令。

(2)We were subjected to very close questioning.

我们受到严厉的盘问。

(3)Have they been subjected to the war?

他们经历过战争吗？

三、思考题

1.《亲历晚清四十五年》一书详细记录了作者在中国长达 45 年传教的

经历。通读全书,如何理解“……他(李提摩太)成为清末大变局中的一位风云人物,在中国近代史上留下了不可磨灭的印记”的观点?

2. 文本中对旅行者代理机构的介绍,对我们了解当时中国的旅行情况具有什么意义?

第九章

北京信札

一、作品导读

萨拉·康格(Sarah Pike Conger),1898年跟随时任美国驻北京公使的丈夫爱德温·赫德·康格(Edwin Hurd Conger,1843—1907)来到中国,并在北京住了7年之久。萨拉·康格作为外交官夫人,有机会到中国各地游玩,也有机会接触晚清时期社会各阶层的人,她甚至有幸觐见慈禧太后,成为和慈禧太后有过密切交往的第一位外交官夫人。

在华期间,萨拉·康格给家人、亲朋好友写了大量的书信。1910年,萨拉·康格将这些书信结集出版,书名定为——*Letters from Peking, with Particular Reference to the Empress Dowager and the Women of China*,中译本题为《北京信札——特别是关于慈禧太后和中国妇女》。《北京信札》里面共收录了80封信件,分别为:致友人11封,致妹妹20封,致侄子17封,致侄女8封,致女儿22封,致姨母1封,致顺王福晋1封。

《北京信札》中不少信件涉及萨拉·康格在中国游玩的经历,这些作品都是她作为一个外国旅行者在中国的所见所闻,既有她感兴趣的中国各地的山川景物、城市城乡建筑、风俗习惯等描写,又有对中国人的生活状况、服饰文化(尤其是女性)、饮食文化等描写,这些作品合在一起如同是一幅勾画晚清社会的全景图,因而《北京信札》成为晚清时期西方来华女性文化游记的代表性作品之一。

《北京信札》反映出作者对中国的情感与态度具有多重性:既有对中国愚昧落后、封闭保守批评的一面,又有对中国人勤劳能干、诚实、冷静、做事精准等特点的褒扬,以及对中国古老文明的赞美;既有对中国被列强入侵的同情,又有对当时她经历过的八国联军入侵中国和企图瓜分中国的事实的欲盖弥彰。

二、作品选读

Episode Ⅰ

LETTERS FROM CHINA

AMERICAN LEGATION, PEKING,

July 23, 1898

We are now in China! Six months ago we were living in our Brazilian Legation, quietly and happily settled, with no thought of leaving beautiful Petropolis. One night the unexpected cablegram came that brought us to the Far East.

If one most appreciates the pleasures of the senses, Brazil is the place to stay; if the pleasures of thought, China is the place to come. It was a cross, at first, to leave our beautiful gardens and the floral hills with their tall trees, luxuriant vines, orchids, ferns, mosses, parasitic plants of many kinds, and rich foliage of vivid colorings. The fruits in Brazil are delicious. Assuredly the five senses can feast in the tropics!

What shall I say of China? My thoughts are battling with one another. Will they ever come to a settlement, so that each may occupy its own province and do its own work? I shall strive for this settlement. Here everything seems beyond the reach of foreigners. China has fortified herself against the outside world as well as against her own people. She is a country of walls. The Great Wall of China is to protect her vast empire; the city and village walls, to protect the collected masses; the palace, compound, cemetery, and temple walls to protect the individual families in their homes, in their worship, and in their unfailing devotion to their ancestors.

Peking, to all appearances, is a city of men. We seldom see the higher or official gentlemen and never the ladies. How I long to go behind these high walls and see something of the Chinese home life! Can it be that good fortune will ever open these locked gates and invite me to enter? I dare not cherish one hope in this direction; the recorded history of more than thirty centuries tells me"No".

Peking is composed of four walled cities: first, the Native City; then the Tartar City, containing the imperial City and the Forbidden City, the latter being within the Imperial.

The Native City is to the south of the Tartar. The Tartar City has massive walls, bastions, heavy gates, and immense gate-towers that can be seen miles away. By paying a few "cash" to the gate-keeper of the ramps, we are permitted to enter and spend leisure hours upon this wall, where we are above the filthy streets and can look down upon the strange scenes. From this height it looks like a vast city-beautiful with "the green things growing".

In the south wall of the Tartar City are three gates, opening into as many broad thoroughfares. The middle gate, or the Ch'ienmen, is the largest and in every way the finest. It is protected by a walled court with four heavy gates. Within this court are two Imperial Temples where, in passing, their Majesties offer prayers and sacrifices. The north gate of this court, which is the Ch'ienmen, leads into the Tartar City, on and on through many gates into the Forbidden City with its beautiful roofs of yellow title. These imperial gateways and the roofs are all we know of this forbidden place. The south gate of this walled court is the "Imperial Gate", through which no one but the Emperor and the Imperial Court is permitted to pass. It looks as though it were never opened. The two other gates opening from this court, one to the east and one to the west, are for the mass of people. Above the south and north gates are massive towers of marble, granite, and brick, with wonderful teak timbers forming giant columns. The Temple of Heaven is at the east and the Temple of Agriculture at the west of the broad street leading south from Imperial

Gate. In special worship the Emperor, "The Son of Heaven," visit these temples. As foreigners are not permitted to enter these high-walled enclosures, all that we can see of these temples is their beautiful capped domes towering above the protecting walls. The "Temple of Heaven", of "Agriculture", the "Sun", "Moon", and "Earth" are national temples and no idols are in them. The finest sacred structure in China is the "Temple of Heaven" in Peking.

While in south America I learned a lesson that is to great help to me here. When I went to Brazil in 1890, I was always comparing and contrasting that country and her people with my country and my people; and to me, mine were always superior. When returning home a year and a half later, I had time on my long journey to review my experiences and look over the thought treasures that I was bearing with me. To my surprise, my treasury was empty. I reflected, seeking the reason for this lack. I soon learned that the attitude of superiority I had taken made it impossible to accumulate anything. When I returned to Brazil, my attitude was changed; I descended from my imaginary height with the determination to seek with open eyes and a willing heart and I was amply rewarded.

Now, in 1898, I have come this far-off land and am somewhat prepared to seek, to see, to detect, to learn, and to bring into my life perhaps a little knowledge of the customs and home life of China and her people.

——Excerpted from *Letters from China*. 1910: 1 – 4. Chicago: A. C. McClurg & Co.

New Words and Expressions

cablegram [ˈkeib(ə)lgræm]n. 海底电报

cross [krɒs]n. 交叉;十字架 vi. &vt. 交叉;杂交;横过 adj. 交叉的;相反的

floral [ˈflɔːr(ə)l]adj. 花的;植物的;植物群的;花似的

luxuriant [lʌg'ʒuəriənt]adj. 繁茂的；丰富的；奢华的；肥沃的

vine [vain]n. 藤；葡萄树；藤本植物 vi. 长成藤蔓；爬藤

orchid ['ɔːkid]n. 兰花；[植] 兰科植物 adj. 淡紫色的

fern [fɜːn]n. [植] 蕨；蕨类植物

moss [mɒs]n. 苔藓；泥沼 vt. 使长满苔藓

parasitic [pærə'sitik]adj. 寄生的

foliage ['fəuliidʒ]n. 植物；叶子(总称)

assuredly [ə'ʃurədli]adv. 确实地；确信地

feast [fiːst]vt. & vi. 享受；款待；宴请 n. 筵席；宴会；节日

fortify ['fɔːtifai]vt. 加强；增强；(酒)的酒精含量；设防于 vi. 筑防御工事

cemetery ['semitri]n. 墓地；公墓

worship ['wɜːʃip]n. 崇拜；礼拜；尊敬 vt. &vi. 崇拜；尊敬；爱慕

cherish ['tʃeriʃ]vt. 珍爱 vt. 怀有(感情等)；抱有(希望等)

bastion ['bæstiən]n. 堡垒；棱堡

ramp [ræmp]n. 斜坡；坡道；敲诈 vi. &vt. 蔓延；狂跳乱撞；敲诈

filthy ['filθi]adj. 肮脏的；污秽的；猥亵的

thoroughfare ['θʌrəfeə]n. 大道；通路

marble ['mɑːb(ə)l]n. 大理石；大理石制品；弹珠 adj. 大理石的；冷酷无情的

granite ['grænit]n. 花岗岩；坚毅；冷酷无情

teak [tiːk]n. 柚木

timber ['timbə]n. 木材；木料

enclosure [in'kləuʒə]n. 附件；围墙；围场

dome [dəum]n. 圆屋顶 vi. 成圆顶状 vt. 加圆屋顶于……上

treasury ['treʒ(ə)ri]n. 国库；金库；财政部；宝库

amply ['æmpli]adv. 充足地；广大地

detect [di'tekt]vt. 察觉；发现；探测

Notes

1. If one most appreciates the pleasures of the senses, Brazil is the

place to stay; if the pleasures of thought, China is the place to come (paragraph 2)：本句话中的 if the pleasures of thought 是 if one most appreciates the pleasures of thought 的省略。

2. Here everything seems beyond the reach of foreigners(paragraph 3)：本句话中的 beyond the reach of 意为"……所不及的"。

如：(1) This is a miracle and a mystery that lies beyond the reach of science.

这是一个超越科学研究的神迹与奥秘。

(2) We don't believe it's beyond the reach of human power.

我们不相信这是人力所做不到的。

Episode Ⅱ

[To A Sister]

Western Hills

August 15, 1898

We sailed from Nagasaki and clean, beautiful Japan, the night of the twentieth of June, passed through the Yellow Sea, and reached Shanghai, China, on the twenty-third. We left our steamship, the Doric, some three miles out in the bay, and with regrets we waved our last good-byes as we sailed out from under her protection. She had been a home to us and seemed like a part of our own dear country. Many times we had gone out into the unknown cities and back again to her as a refuge.

We remained in Shanghai eight days, but were only in the foreign concession. This concession is a modification of both the Far East and the West. I never saw men work before! They do the work of beasts and are treated like beasts. China is thickly populated and the people cry out against any device that takes labor and support from their poor coolie classes.

The Taotai of Shanghai made his official call, entertaining us later at a dinner which was half Chinese and half foreign, the courses alternating. The Chinese food was served in Chinese dishes and eaten with chopsticks, while the foreign food was served in strictly foreign style. The Taotai speaks English well, and so does his secretary, who was educated in America. Toasts of welcome were given. The Taotai's wife was not present; in explanation he said, "My people do not approve."

We reached Tientsin on Independence Day. The American consul and his wife held a reception, thus happily remembering our country's birthday. We came by rail to Peking, or rather to the station five miles from the city. Three members of the Legation met us with sedan chairs, Peking carts, and the necessary mafoos, outriders, coolies, and baggage-carts. Our procession was formed, and we started for Peking.

China seems to be one vast graveyard. Many, many graves, anywhere and everywhere, lay along our route to the city. After entering the gate of the Native City we still had quite a journey before reaching the Tartar City. Many of the streets were crowded with men. China surely is the country of the "blue gown." We at last reached the wall of the American Legation compound and enter the large gate, where Colonel Denby, the American Minister, met us. We had reached what was to be our home! It was not prepossessing; the compound, however, was quite, clean, and green. As we looked out of our windows and doors, it seemed almost as though we were looking into the woods. This was refreshing. A "compound" is a walled enclosure divided into courts with buildings. We remained in the American Legation compound three weeks before coming to the Hills.

——Excerpted from *Letters from China*. 1910: 4 – 5. Chicago: A. C. McClurg & Co.

New Words and Expressions

steamship ['stiːmʃip]n. 轮船；汽船

refuge ['refjuːdʒ]n. 避难；避难所 vi. & vt. 避难；逃避

concession [kən'seʃ(ə)n]n. 让步；特许(权)；承认；退位

modification [mɒdifi'keiʃ(ə)n]n. 修改；修正；改变

alternating ['ɔːltəneitiŋ]adj. 交替的；交互的

consul ['kɒns(ə)l]n. 领事；(古罗马的)两执政官之一

legation [li'geiʃ(ə)n]n. 公使馆；使者的派遣

mafoo [mɑ:fu:]马夫(汉语音译)

outrider ['ɑʊtraidə]n. 先驱者；摩托车警卫；骑马侍从

procession [prə'seʃ(ə)n]n. 队伍；行列 vi. 列队行进

graveyard ['grevjɑrd]n. 墓地

quit [kwit]vt. 离开；放弃；停止 vi. 离开；辞职；停止 n. 离开

Episode Ⅲ

[TO A NEPHEW]

WESTERN HILLS

September 15, 1898

September 13. What an experience! The crowing of the cocks, the braying of the many donkeys, the bleating of the sheep, the constant ringing of the bells worn by the moving, laden camels in the endless caravan, filled the air with dream melody all unreal to us the night through.

After a good breakfast we were off for the Great Wall of China, fourteen miles away. We left the carts at Nankou until our return. The ride through the Nankou pass was most delightful. It was up, up, up, all the way, climbing a mountainous road which was, however, broad and well kept. On one side were sheer cliffs, on the other a rocky river-bed with its clear rippling stream. Such a happy ride! On our way we saw many hundreds of fine camels; these camels rest during the day and travel with their packs at night. The prosperity of the country was shown by the flocks of sheep, in the hundreds of mules laden with wool, hides, tea, fruits, grain, fodder, cotton, and other commodities. We met pack-cattle from Mongolia with red-faced Mongol drivers. We also met a number of mule litters, a few carts drawn by mules, and many men riding on donkeys. All were bent on business, and we were forcibly impressed with the fact that the Chinese do not seek their pleasure in travel. This well-kept road is a direct pass over the mountains from Peking to Mongolia and Russia. Most of the roads that we have traveled in China have been poorly kept. The highways are mostly footpaths, which are sufficient for Chinese travel.

We reached the Great Wall at ten o'clock, climbed to the top, then walked, and climbed on and on, up and down, until we reached an elevation where we could catch a fine view of the mountains and of this wonderful coiling, climbing, leaping thing. This Wall is wonderful indeed! It speaks of great engineering, great labor, great time, great expense, and patience without end. Its endurance tells much of the thought that was put into it; thought symbolical of protection, unity, strength. This Great Wall of China was built more than two hundred years before the birth of Jesus Christ, and the work was finished in ten years. Think of it, over two thousand years ago! It begins at Shan-hai Kwan by the sea and climbs over the mountains, across the northern boundary of China proper, until it reaches the desert of Gobi, north of Tibet. It is fifteen hundred miles long, about thirty-five feet wide, and varies in height from thirty to fifty feet. The facings are of brick several feet in thickness, the interjacent shell being filled with stone and earth stamped solid; it is surmounted with a paving of brick similar to that of the facing. It is said that it took an army of three hundred thousand men to protect the builders, and more than a million men to build the wall. But your encyclopedia will tell you all this—why should I go on?

Three monuments remain to remind the generations that the Emperor Ch'in Shih was a great man: first, the Great Wall of China, which he built; second, the title Huang-ti for Emperor, which he was the first to adopt; third, the name China. Still this man is remembered in China as a burner of books and a murderer of scholars, rather than as builder of this wonderfully aged wall, or founder of this immense and long-standing empire. We ate our picnic tiffin in one of the towers upon the Wall, and later we went through the gate into Mongolia, against which China was fortified. As we sat on the rocks in Mongolia musing and looking upon that aged, yet well-preserved, wall structure, and tried to realize that men over two thousand years ago walked upon that soil, made and placed those steadfast bricks, we were brought back to the "now."

——**Excerpted from *Letters from China*. 1910:12 - 14. Chicago:A. C. McClurg & Co.**

New Words and Expressions

bray [brei]vi. &vt. 叫;捣碎叫 n. 驴叫声;喇叭声
bleat [bliːt]vi. &vt 咩咩叫;胡扯;抱怨 n. 咩咩叫声
laden ['leid(ə)n]adj. 负载的;装满的;苦恼的 vt. 装载(等于 lade)
fodder ['fɒdə]n. 饲料;素材 vt. 喂
witch [witʃ]n. 巫婆;女巫 vt. 迷惑;施巫术
tiffin ['tifin]n. 午餐

三、思考题

1. 读完节选文本,如何理解作者以下的观点:"...If one most appreciates the pleasures of the senses, Brazil is the place to stay; if the pleasures of thought, China is the place to come..."

2. 在对中国万里长城的描写时,作者表达的是对中国怎样的评价?

第十章

徒步穿越中国:1909—1910
一个英国人的中国旅行记

一、作品导读

埃德温·约翰·丁格尔(Edwin John Dingle,1881—1972),中文名为丁乐梅,出生于英国康沃尔郡,1921年定居美国加州。丁乐梅是一位长期在中国从事传教工作的传教士、新闻工作者、出版商、作家、旅行家,同时也是精神意念治疗法(Mentalphysics,又曰“超级瑜伽”)的创始人。丁乐梅自幼对东方尤其是中国有极大的兴趣,在中国与印度旅居20余年,并拍下了大量珍贵的照片,著有涉及文学、哲学和地理学等领域的作品《辛亥革命目击记——〈大陆报〉特派员的现场报道》《徒步穿越中国:1909—1910一个英国人的中国旅行记》《我在西藏的生活》《永恒的边陲:拥抱“徒步神州”》《另类呼吸让生命重生》《精神意念科学治疗法》等14部。

丁乐梅在中国生活了21年(1906—1926),先后被聘为《字林西报》的记者和上海英文《大陆报》的特派记者。《徒步穿越中国:1909—1910一个英国人的中国旅行记》是100多年前他在中国西南地区徒步期间(1909年3月4日—1910年2月14日)用打字机撰写的游记,该书从生态、民俗、社会变革、社会思潮等多个角度记录了沿途的风土人情,途中他还拍摄了大量的照片,此次旅行和该书被誉为“跨越百年的冒险之旅,末日帝国的终极记录”。

《徒步穿越中国:1909—1910一个英国人的中国旅行记》记录的旅行始于1909年3月,丁乐梅为了实现“从中国内部好好观察一下这个国家”的愿望,从新加坡经法属西贡(今越南胡志明市)抵达上海,途经南京、宜昌、重庆、宜宾、昭通、昆明、楚雄、大理、腾冲等地，其旅行线路如今已不可复制，尤其在云南境内许多条件恶劣、人烟稀少的地带，他坚持不坐轿、不骑马，与雇来的中国苦力一起徒步穿越。此次旅行异常艰苦，丁乐梅在克服语言障碍、道路艰难、食宿低劣、伤病侵袭、暴动袭击等多重困难之后（也因病几乎死于云南），他终于凭借自己的意志力，在朋友和中国人的帮助下走完这段旅程，最终在 1910 年 2 月离开中国进入英属缅甸。

丁乐梅在这本书中表达了他对中国壮丽山川的深深眷恋，尤其是关于云南的壮丽风景、民俗风情的描写占了很大的篇幅，他将云南称为“华西的瑞士”，认为任何一个自然爱好者都可以在这里找到回家的感觉。同时，他在书中坚信中国这头睡狮拥有巨大的潜力，他在当时就颇有远见地认为中国若能进一步对外开放，日后一定会在国际上占有重要地位。

以下节选的是其在四川和云南途中的旅行见闻文章。

二、作品选读

Episode Ⅰ

The rather extreme idea of walking across this Flowery Land came to me early in the year 1909, although for many years I had cherished the hope of seeing Interior China ere modernity had robbed her and her wonderful people of their isolation and antediluvianism, and ever since childhood my interest in China has always been considerable. A little prior to the China New Year, a friend of mine dined with me at my rooms in Singapore, in the Straits Settlements, and the conversation about China resulted in our decision then and there to travel through the Empire on holiday. He, because at the time he had little else to do; the author, because he thought that a few months' travel in mid-China would, from a journalistic standpoint, be passed profitably, the intention being to arrive home in dear old England late in the summer of the same year.

We agreed to cross China on foot, and accordingly on February 22, 1909, just as the sun was sinking over the beautiful harbor of Singapore—that most valuable strategic Gate of the Far East, where Crown Colonial administration, however, is allowed by a lethargic British Government to become more and more bungled every year—we settled down on board the French mail steamer Nera, bound for Shanghai. My friends, good fellows, in reluctantly speeding me on my way, prophesied that this would prove to be my last long voyage to a last long rest, that the Chinese would never allow me to come out of China alive. Such is the ignorance of the average man concerning the conditions of life and travel in the interior of this Land of Night.

Here, then, was I on my way to that land towards which all the world was straining its eyes, whose nation, above all nations of the earth, was altering for better things, and coming out of its historic shell. "Reform, reform, reform," was the echo, and I myself was on the way to hear it.

At the time I started for China, the cry of "China for the Chinese" was heard in all countries, among all peoples. Statesmen were startled by it, editors wrote the phrase to death, magazines were filled with copy—good, bad and indifferent—mostly written, be it said, by men whose knowledge of the question was by no means complete: editorial opinion, and contradiction of that opinion, were printed side by side in journals having a good name. To one who endeavoured actually to understand what was being done, and whither these broad tendencies and strange cravings of the Chinese were leading a people who formerly were so indifferent to progress, it seemed essential that he should go to the country, and there on the spot, make a study of the problem.

Was the reform, if genuine at all, universal in China? Did it reach to the ends of the Empire?

That a New China had come into being, and was working astounding results in the enlightened provinces above the Yangtze and those connected with the capital by railway, was common knowledge; but one found it hard to believe that the west and the south-west of the empire were moved by the same spirit of Europeanism, and it will be seen that China in the west moves, if at all, but at a snail's pace: the second part of this volume deals with that portion of the subject.

——**Excerpted from *Across China on Foot*. 1911: 3 – 6. New York: Henry Holt & Company.**

New Words and Expressions

ere [eə]prep. & conj. 在……以前;毋宁

journalistic [dʒɜːnəˈlistik]adj. 新闻业的;新闻工作者的

lethargic [liˈθɑːdʒik]adj. 昏睡的;无生气的

bungle [ˈbʌŋgl]vt. & vi. 笨手笨脚地做 n. 粗劣;失败;笨拙

prophesy [ˈprɒfisai]vt. & vi. 预言;预告;传教

contradiction [kɒntrəˈdikʃ(ə)n]n. 矛盾;否认;反驳

whither [ˈwiðə]ɑdv. 到哪里 conj. 无论到何种程度;无论到哪里

craving [ˈkreiviŋ]n. 渴望;热望

Europeanism [juərəˈpiːənizəm]n. 欧洲主义;欧洲风气

Notes

Here, then, was I on my way to that land towards which all the world was straining its eyes (paragraph 3):此句为倒装句，强调状语。为了保持句子的平衡或为了强调表语和状语，或使上下文紧密衔接，把它们放在句首用倒装句。

如:(1) East of the town lies a beautiful lake.

小镇东头有个美丽的湖。

(2) Outside the doctor's clinic were twenty patients.

诊所外面有 20 个病人。

Episode Ⅱ

Upon arrival at Kweifu one bids farewell to the Gorges. This town, formerly a considerable coaling centre, overlooks magnificently pretty hillocks, with cottage gardens cultivated in every accessible corner, and a wide sweep of the river.

We landed with difficulty. "Chor, chor!" yelled the trackers, who marked time to their cry, swinging their arms to and fro at each shot step; but they almost gave up the ghost. However, we did land, and so did our boy, who bought excellent provisions and meat, which, alas! too soon disappeared. The mutton and beef gradually grew less and daily blackened, wrapped up in opposite corners of the cabin, under the protection from the wet of a couple of sheets of the "Pink' Un".

From Kweifu to Wan Hsian there was the same kind of scenery—the clear river winding among sand-flats and gravel-banks, with occasional stiff rapids. But after having been in a wu-pan for several days, suffering that which has been detailed, and much besides, the journey got a bit dreary. These, however, are ordinary circumstances; but when one has been laid up on a bench of a bed for three days with a high temperature, a legacy of several years in the humid tropics, the physical discomfort baffles description. Malaria, as all sufferers know, has a tendency to cause trouble as soon as one gets into cold weather, and in my case, as will be seen in subsequent parts of this book, it held faithfully to its best traditions. Fever on the Yangtze in a wu-pan would require a chapter to itself, not to mention the kindly eccentricities of a companion whose knowledge of malaria was most elementary and whose knowledge of nursing absolutely nil. But I refrain. As also do I of further talk about the Yangtze gorges and the rapids.

From Kweifu to Wan Hsian is a tedious journey. The country opens out, and is more or less monotonously flat. The majority of the dangers and difficulties, however, are over, and one is able to settle down in comparative peace. Fortunately for the author, nothing untoward happened, but travelers are warned not to be too sanguine. Wrecks have happened within a few miles of the destination, generally to be accounted for by the unhappy knack the Chinese boatman has of taking all precautions where the dangerous rapids exist, and leaving all to chance elsewhere. Some two years later, as I was coming down the river from Chung-king in December, I counted no less than nine wrecks, one boat having on board a cargo for the China Inland Mission authorities of no less than 480 boxes. The contents were spread out on the banks to dry, while the boat was turned upside down and repaired on the spot.

——**Excerpted from *Across China on Foot*. 1911: 43 - 44. New York: Henry Holt & Company.**

New Words and Expressions

hillock [ˈhilək]n. 小丘;小山似的一堆
to and fro 来回地
gravel [ˈgræv(ə)l]n. 碎石;砂砾 vt. 用碎石铺
dreary [ˈdriəri]adj. 沉闷的;枯燥的
baffle [ˈbæfl]vt. 使……困惑;使……受挫折 n. 挡板;困惑
malaria [məˈleəriə]n. 疟疾;瘴气
eccentricity [eksenˈtrisiti]n. 古怪;怪癖
monotonous [məˈnɒt(ə)nəs]adj. 单调的;无抑扬顿挫的;无变化的
sanguine [ˈsæŋgwin]adj. 乐观的;满怀希望的;面色红润的

Episode Ⅲ

As one meanders through the country, watching a people who are equaled nowhere in the world for their industry, plodding away over the worst roads any civilized country possesses, he cannot but think, even looking at the question from the Chinaman's standpoint so far as he is able, that, were free scope once given for the infusion of Western energy and methods into an active, trade-loving people like the Chinese, China would rival the United States in wealth and natural resources. The Chinaman knows that his country, the natural resources of the country and the people, will allow him to do things on a scale which will by and by completely overbalance the doings of countries less favored by Nature than his own. He knows that when properly developed his country will be one of the richest in the world, yet even when he is filled with such ideas he is just as cunctative as he has ever been. He has got the idea that he should not commence to exhaust the wealth of his country before it is absolutely necessary.

Above all, he has now made up his mind that he himself, unaided by the foreigner, is going to develop it just as he likes and just when he likes.

The day of the foreign concession is gone. The Chinaman now is paddling his own canoe, and it is only by cultivating his friendship, by proving to him by acts, and not by words, that the intrusion of privileged enterprises—such as great mining concessions and railway concessions, in which the foreigner demands that he the only principal—is no longer contemplated, that the day will be won. But it is equally true that only by combining European and Chinese interests on the modern company system, the real Opening of China can be effected.

——Excerpted from *Across China on Foot*. 1911: 86 - 87. New York: Henry Holt & Company.

New Words and Expressions

meander [miˈændə]n. 漫步；曲流 vt. &vi. 漫步；漫谈

plod [plɒd]vi. 辛勤工作；沉重地走 vt. 沉重缓慢地走

infusion [inˈfjuːʒ(ə)n]n. 灌输；浸泡；注入物；激励

overbalance [əuvəˈbæl(ə)ns]n. 超额；超量；不平衡 vi. 失去平衡

connotative [ˈkɔnəuteitiv]adj. 内涵的；隐含的；含蓄的

commence [kəˈmens]v. 开始；着手

paddle [ˈpædl]n. 划桨；明轮翼 vt. 拌；搅；用桨划

canoe [kəˈnuː]n. 独木舟；轻舟 vi. 乘独木舟

contemplate [ˈkɒntempleit]vt. 沉思；注视；思忖 vi. 冥思苦想

Notes

...he cannot but think, even looking at the question from the Chinaman's standpoint so far as he is able (paragraph 1):此处"cannot but +动词"结构表示"禁不住……"。

如:(1) I cannot but laugh.

我不禁笑了起来。

(2)I cannot but admire his courage.

我不得不佩服他的勇气。

Episode Ⅳ

Often, gazing over the sunlit landscape, in this land "South of the Clouds," one is held spellbound by the intense beauty of this little-known province, and one wonders what all this grand scenery, untouched and unmarred by the hand of man, would become were it in the centre of a continent covered by the ubiquitous globe-trotter.

No country in the world more than West China possesses mountains of combined majesty and grace. Rocks, everywhere arranged in masses of a rude and gigantic character, have a ruggedness tempered by a singular airiness of form and softness of environment, in a climate favorable in some parts to the densest vegetation, and in others wild and barren. One is always in sight of mountains rising to fourteen thousand feet or more, and constantly scaling difficult pathways seven or eight or nine thousand feet above the sea. And in the loneliness of a county where nothing has altered very much the handiwork of god, an awe-inspiring silence pervades everything. Bold, grey cliffs shoot up here through a mass of verdure and of foliage, and there white cottages, perched in seemingly inaccessible positions, glisten in the sun on the colored mountain-sides. You saunter through stony hollows, along straight passes, traversed by torrents, overhung by high walls of rocks, now winding through broken, shaggy chasms and huge, wandering fragments, now suddenly emerging into some emerald valley, where peace, long established, seems to repose sweetly in the bosom of Strength. Everywhere beauty alternates wonderfully with grandeur. Valleys close in abruptly, intersected by huge mountain masses, the stony water-worn ascent of which is hardly passable.

Yes, Yunnan is imperatively a country first of mountains, then of lakes. The scenery, embodying truly Alpine magnificence with the minute sylvan beauty of Killarney or of Devonshire, is nowhere excelled in the length and breadth of the Empire.

——**Excerpted from *Across China on Foot*. 1911: 171 – 172. New York: Henry Holt & Company.**

New Words and Expressions

spellbound ['spelbaʊnd]adj. 被咒语所镇住的;出神的;被迷住的

unmarred [ʌn'mɑːd]adj. 未损伤的;未玷污的

ubiquitous [juː'bikwitəs]adj. 普遍存在的;无所不在的

globe-trotter 周游世界者

ruggedness ['rʌgidnis]n. 强度;坚固性;险峻;崎岖

airiness ['eərinis]n. 通风;空虚;微妙

scaling ['skeliŋ]n. 缩放比例;刮治术

handiwork ['hændiwɜːk]n. 手工艺;手工制品;行为后果

awe-inspiring ['ɔːin, spaiəriŋ]adj. 使人敬畏的;令人惊叹的

verdure ['vɜːdjə]n. 碧绿

glisten ['glisn]vi. 闪光;闪亮 n. 闪光;闪耀

saunter ['sɔːntə]n. 漫步;闲逛 vi. 闲逛;漫步

traverse ['trævəs]n. 穿过 vt. & vi. 穿过;来回移动

shaggy ['ʃægi]adj. 蓬松的;表面粗糙的

chasm ['kæzəm]n. 峡谷;裂口;分歧;深坑

sylvan ['silvən]adj. 森林的;农村的

三、思考题

1. 如何理解“同时我也不禁怀疑，上述的一切是否会随着中国的开放而覆灭？”

2. 身处“云之南端”，作者称“全中国再无风景可以超越这里”。你对此观点如何评价？

3.《徒步穿越中国》一书被称为是“跨越百年的冒险之旅，末日帝国的终极记录”。你对此观点如何评价？

第十一章

扬子江流域及以外地区

一、作品导读

伊莎贝拉·伯德(Isabella Lucy Bird Bishop, Mrs. Bishop,1831—1904),英国维多利亚时代最著名的女性旅行家。伯德毕生钟情于异国旅行,她22岁开始到世界各地旅行,足迹遍布北美、中东和亚洲等地,旅行期间写了大量的游记作品,因她无畏的冒险精神和在地理考察方面的贡献,她成为英国皇家地理学会第一位女会员,代表作有11卷本《伊莎贝拉·伯德游记全集》(*Collected travel writings of Isabella Bird*)。

1896年,时年65岁的伯德来到中国,此时她身患血脂性心脏衰弱、肺部感染、痛风、周期性脊柱痿弱等多种疾病,但她以惊人的毅力完成了历时15个月、全程5千多英里的长江流域及川藏地区的旅行,旅行结束后回到英国。她根据日记和随笔写下了数十万字的考察游记——《扬子江流域及以外地区》。在100多年前交通不便的情况下,伯德这位柔弱平凡的外国女性在中国所经历的旅行不能不说是一个令人钦佩的壮举。

《扬子江流域及以外地区》(又译为《1898:一个英国女人眼中的中国》)比较详细记录了伯德在长江及川藏地区的旅行线路与经历,大致可以分为7个部分:(1—3章)乘当地人的木船从上海到杭州,经绍兴、宁波又返回上海;(4—9章)乘外国轮船从上海经镇江、芜湖、九江至汉口,再由汉口经沙市到宜昌;(10—16章)乘帆船从宜昌起行,穿过壮丽的长江三峡,经奉节(夔府)、云阳到达万县;(17—28章)从万县走陆路经梁平(梁山县)、渠县、营山、南部到达阆中(保宁府),再经苍溪、剑阁、梓潼、绵阳、彭县、灌县到达成都;(29—34章)灌县经汶川(威州、理番厅)、理县(杂谷脑)、米亚罗到达马尔康的梭磨,再返回成都;(35—37章)由成都乘"乌榜船"沿岷江顺流而下,经眉山、乐山(嘉定府)、宜宾(叙府)、泸州到达重庆;最后一段是在重庆坐船回上海。

作为一位晚清时期西方来华女性旅行者的代表人物,伯德在《扬子江流域及以外地区》中用一种冷静、理性、客观的态度看待沿途的风光古迹与民风民俗,体现出她与众不同的、敏锐的观察力。全书以作者旅行行踪为线索,在记叙中夹杂议论,文笔优美、情感真挚,尤其是书中对长江三峡和川藏地区的壮丽风光描写,让读者心向往之。有人评价该书向世界"传达了这个国家及其人民的真实印象",是"十九世纪末,一本最耀眼的,彻底证明中国价值的书"。

以下节选的是伯德到达上海,以及在四川、川藏地区旅行经历的文章。

二、作品选读

Episode Ⅰ

I arrived in Shanghai the first time on a clear, bright autumn day. The sky was very blue, and the masses of exotic trees, the green, shaven lawns, the belated roses, and the clumps of chrysanthemums in the fine public gardens gave a great charm to the first view of the settlement. Two big, lofty, white hulks for bonded Indian opium are moored permanently in front of the gardens. Gunboats and larger war-vessels of all nations, all painted white, and the fine steamers of the Messageries Maritimes have their moorings a little higher up. Boats, with crews in familiar uniforms, and covered native boats gaily painted, the latter darting about like dragon-flies, were playing ceaselessly, and as it was the turn of the tide, hundreds of junks were passing seawards under their big brown sails.

On landing at the fine landing-stage, where kind friends received me and took me to the British Consul's residence in the spacious grounds of the Consulate, I was at once impressed with the exquisite dress of the ladies, who were at least a half of the throng, and with the look of wealth and comfort which prevails.

All along the British bund, for at least a mile from the Soochow Creek, which separates it from Hongkew, to the French settlement, are banks, hongs, hotels, and private houses of the most approved and massive Anglo-Oriental architecture, standing in large, shady gardens, the Hong Kong and Shanghai Bank, the "P. & O." office, the Canadian-Pacific Railroad office, the fine counting-house and dwelling-house of the old and famous firm of Jardine, Matheson & Co., and the long facade of the British Consular buildings, with their wide sweep of lawns, being prominent.

The broad carriage-road and fine flagged side-walk are truly cosmopolitan. Well-dressed men and women of all civilized nations, and of some which are not civilized, promenade gaily on the walk and in the garden. Single and two-horse carriages and buggies, open and closed, with coachmen and grooms in gay and often fantastic cotton liveries, dash along the drive. Hackney victorias abound, and there are jinrickshas (from which foreigners drop the first syllable) in hundreds, with Chinese runners, and Shanghai wheelbarrows innumerable, some loaded with goods or luggage, while the coolies of others are trundling along from two to four Chinese men or women of the lower classes seated on matted platforms on either side of the wheel, facing forwards.

I was not prepared for the Chinese element being so much an evidence in the foreign settlement. It is not only that clerks and compradors dressed in rich silks on which the characters for happiness and longevity and the symbols of luck are brocaded are in numbers on the bund, and that all the servile classes, as may be expected, are Chinese, but that Chinese shops of high standing, such as Laou Kai Fook's, are taking their place in fine streets which run back from the bund, that some of the handsomest carriage on the bund and the Bubbling Well Road, the fashionable afternoon drive of Shanghai, are owned and filled with Chinese, that Chinese ladies and children richly dressed drive in the same fashion, and that of late, specially, wealthy Chinese have become keen competitors for British houses, and have even outbid foreigners for them. Is Shanghai menaced by the "Yellow Peril" as Malacca, Singapore, and Penang have been?

A great trading Chinese city, with an estimated population of 200, 000, has grown up within the foreign boundary, subject to foreign municipal laws and sanitary regulations, but so absolutely Chinese, that were it not for the wide streets and the absence of the refuse-heaps and bad smells, one might think oneself in one of the great cities of the interior. The Chinese are quite capable of appreciating the comfort and equity of foreign rule, and the various advantages which they enjoy under it. They pay municipal taxes according to their rating, and "duty for their Land", which it is usual for them to hold in the name of a foreigner. They are under the jurisdiction of the Chinese Government, but civil cases in which foreigners are concerned and breaches of the peace are tried in what is known as the "Mixed Court," an apparently satisfactory and workable arrangement, and serious criminal cases belong to the Chinese Shanghai magistrate.

——**Excerpted from *The Yangtze Valley and Beyond*. 1899: 17 – 19. London: John Murray.**

New Words and Expressions

shaven [ˈʃeivn]adj. 刮过脸的;修过脸的;削发的
belated [biˈleitid]adj. 迟来的;误期的
clump [klʌmp]n. 土块 vi. 形成一丛 vt. 使凝结成块
chrysanthemum [kriˈsænθəməm]n. 菊花
bonded [ˈbɒndid]adj. 有担保的;存入保税仓库的
opium [ˈəʊpiəm]n. 鸦片;麻醉剂 adj. 鸦片的
moor [mɔː]vt. 系住;使停泊 n. 沼泽;荒野
consulate [ˈkɑnsələt]n. 领事;领事馆;领事任期
cosmopolitan [ˈkɑzməˈpɑlətn]adj. 世界性的;世界主义的 n. 世界主义者
promenade [prɑməˈneid]n. 漫步;公共散步场所;滨海步行大道
buggy [ˈbʌgi]n. 童车;双轮单座轻马车 adj. 多虫的

livery ['livəri]n. 制服;侍从 adj. 有肝病症状的

jinricksha [d'ʒinrikʃə]n. 人力车;网络黄包车

wheelbarrow ['wi:l'bærəʊ]n. 独轮手推车; 小车;用手推车运

cooly ['ku:li]n. 苦力(特指东方的廉价劳动力)

trundle ['trʌnd(ə)l]v. 滚动;沉重缓慢地走

comprador [ˌkɒmprə'dɔ:]n. (旧时中国的)买办

longevity [lɔn'dʒɛvəti]n. 长寿;长命;寿命

outbid [ˌaʊt'bid]vt. 在开价上战胜;出价高于

menace ['menəs]n. 威胁;恐吓 vi. & vt. 恐吓;进行威胁

sanitary ['sænit(ə)ri]adj. 卫生的;清洁的 n. 公共厕所

jurisdiction [ˌdʒʊris'dikʃən]n. 司法权;审判权;管辖权;权力

magistrate ['mædʒis'tret]n. 地方法官;文职官员

Notes

that were it not for the wide streets and the absence of the refuse-heaps and bad smells, one might think (paragraph 6):此处"were it not for"为虚拟语气，是对现在或将来的虚拟，意思是"如果没有""要不是由于"。在 if 条件从句中，如果含有 were，should，had 等动词，则可以通过主谓倒装的方法来取消连接词 if，从而变成无连接词条件从句。在正式语体中，if it were not for 可以写成无连词的形式:were it not for。

如:(1) Were it not for your help, I would still be homeless.

要是没有你的帮助，我仍然会无家可归。

(2) They might live quite comfortably were it not for a quarrel with their next door neighbor.

他们如果没有和邻居吵架，可能会过得很舒服。

Episode Ⅱ

The following day was misty, grey, and grim, and several of its successors were much like it. One of the local names of SZE CHUAN is

"The Cloudy Province." Kind, capable Mr. Thompson retuned to Wan after giving the coolies various instructions intended for my benefit; and form thenceforth I depended on myself. The great event of the day was the complete change in Be-dien as soon as I was bereft of Europeans. His pride and temper always remained, and were liable to flare up, or die down into a mephitic stare of sullenness, but from that morning till I left China he was active and attentive, was never without leave out of hearing of my whistle, was always at hand to help me over slippery and difficult places, showed great pluck, never grumbled, arranged and packed up my things, interpreted carefully, improved daily in English, always contrived to get hot water and food for me, and the whole made a tolerable travelling servant.

The travelling was without fatigue. I walked when it suited me, and for the rest might have been in an easy-chair in a drawing-room. The chair-bearers were energetic, and their "boss," a great wag, kept them constantly laughing. Their good-nature never failed. One day when, to relieve them, I walked up a long flight of stairs over a pass, they asked, "Does the foreign woman think we are not strong enough to carry her?" The idea of a wish to be kind to them never entered their heads, yet we gradually came to understand each other a little; and I found my cloak put over my shoulders for me, a wooden stool brought for my feet, Sunday little comforts attended to, and a growing interest in photography, reaching the extent of pointing out objects at times "to make pictures of"! By the end of the second day they had all shaken into my "ways", and things went very smoothly.

The day's routine was a cup of tea and some flour stirabout at seven; but, though I was always ready and eager to start at eight, it was usually half-past, and often nine, before we got off. The coolies' first breakfast was often late, and there was the haggling about the bill, neither side liking to give in. It was only a shilling for the board and lodging for myself and my servant! This included his supper and breakfast, my rice, and a room to myself, his share of the coolies' room, an iron lamp fixed on the wall, with an oil well and a wick in a spout encrusted with the soot and grime of years, and if I had a charcoal brazier, the charge was a farthing more. My other travelling expenses came 4s. 6d a day; 5s. 6d. covered everything, including a fowl for curry every third day.

My bearers trudged along at an even pace, stopping two or three times for a drink and smoke at tea shops where others congregated, until the halt for dinner at a restaurant of more pretensions, outside of which I sat in my chair in the village street, the unwilling centre of a large and very dirty crowd, which had leisure to stand round me for an hour, staring, making remarks, laughing at my peculiarities, pressing closer and closer till there was hardly air to breathe, taking out my hairpins, and passing my gloves round and putting them on their dirty hands, on two occasions abstracting my spoon and slipping it into their sleeves, being in no wise abased when they were detected. For at first I ate a little cold rice, but wearying of being a spectacle, and being convinced that as a general rule our insular habit is to eat too much, I gave up this moderate lunch, and contented myself with a morsel of chocolate eaten surreptitiously. On the occasions when the villagers wearied of their entertainment, even of gloves, which they thought were worn to conceal some desperate skin disease, and dropped off, small black pigs, with upright rows of bristles on their lean, curved spines, timidly took their place with expectations which were not realized, picking about, even under the poles of the chair, for fragments which they did not find, and even nibbling my straw shoes, and ancient and long-legged poultry were as odiously familiar.

When they had fed and smoked, the men shouldered their burdens, and trudged on till about sunset, stopping, as in the morning, for smokes and drinks, I walking and photographing as it suited me. Sometimes we put up at a wayside inn, without even the privacy of a yard; this was in very small places, where the curiosity was not so overwhelming.

In towns the case was different. The inn yard was often enclosed by planking and a wide door, within which there might be one, two, or three courts, possibly with flowers in pots and a little gaudy paint. Some of these inns accommodate over 200 travelers, with their baggage. Every room is full, and between money-changing, eating, "sing-song," and gambling, and half-naked waiters rushing about with small trays, and numbers of men all shouting together, it is pretty lively. At the extreme end of the establishment is the "kuan's room," with one for attendants on each side. The crowd which always gathered during my passage down the street rolled in at the doorway, blocking up the yard, shouting, often times hooting, and fighting each other for a look at the foreigner. Fortunately doors in Chinese inns have strong wooden bolts, and when my baggage and I were once ensconced I was secure from intrusion, unless a few men and boys had on ahead to take possession of the room before I entered it, or forced themselves in behind Be-dien when he brought my dinner. If it were merely a boarded wall, a row of patient eyes usually watched me for an hour, and with much gratification, for these rooms are dark with the door shut, and my candle revealed my barbarian proceedings.

——**Excerpted from *The Yangtze Valley and Beyond*. 1899:207 - 209. London:John Murray.**

New Words and Expressions

bereft [bi'reft]adj. 丧失的;被剥夺的 v. 失去……的(bereave 的过去式)
mephitic [me'fitik]adj. 有毒的;有恶臭的;毒气的
grumble ['grʌmbl]vi. 抱怨;嘟囔 n. 怨言
contrive [kən'traiv]vt. 设计;发明;图谋 vi. 谋划
cloak [kləʊk]n. 斗篷;宽大外衣;托词 vt. 遮掩;隐匿
haggle ['hægl]n. 讨价还价;争论 vt. & vi. 乱劈;争论
encrust [in'krʌst]vt. 包上外壳;装饰外层 vi. 结壳
soot [sʊt]n. 煤烟;烟灰 vt. 用煤烟熏黑
grime [graim]n. 尘垢;污点;煤尘 vt. 使污秽;使……弄脏
brazier ['breziə˞]n. 火盆;铜匠(等于 brasier)
farthing ['fɑːðiŋ]n. 一点儿;极少量
congregate ['kɒŋgrigeit]vt. & vi. 聚集
insular ['insələ˞]adj. 孤立的;与世隔绝的;海岛的

morsel [ˈmɔrsl]n. 一口；(食物)少量

surreptitiously [sʌrəpˈtiʃəsli]adv. 偷偷地；秘密地；不正当地

spine [spain]n. 脊柱；脊椎；刺；书脊

nibble [ˈnibl]v. 一点一点地吃；谨慎地着手；吹毛求疵

poultry [ˈpəultri]n. 家禽

plank [plæŋk]n. [木] 厚木板；支架 vt. 在……上铺板；撂下

hoot [huːt]n. 鸣响；嘲骂声 vi. 鸣响；大声叫嚣 vt. 轰赶；呵斥

Notes

1. The idea of a wish to be kind to them never entered their heads, yet we gradually came to understand each other a litter (paragraph 2)：此句"yet"用作连词时，与 but 一样也主要用于转折，意为"但是；而"。

如：(1) I have failed, yet I shall try again.

我失败了，但我还要尝试。

(2) He said he was our friend, yet he wouldn't help us.

他说他是我们的朋友，但却不肯帮助我们。

2. this was in very small places, where the curiosity was not so overwhelming (paragraph 5)：此处"where"用作关系副词，引导定语从句。

如：(1) England is one of the few countries where people drive on the left.

英国是少数沿左侧开车的国家之一。

(2) We then moved to Paris, where we lived for six years.

我们后来搬到巴黎，在那里住了 6 年。

Episode Ⅲ

The scanty hoar frost lay on the ground at five the next morning, and the sun rose, as he had set, in glory, flooding the canyons with a deluge of amber light. There was a considerable delay before starting, and to the last I feared the wiles of Chinese officialism; but it turned out to be only the usual difficulty of the first start with animals—weighing and adjusting loads and the like. There were three strong, whole-backed, pleasant-faced red mules, and the muleteer was equally pleasant, a Man-tze lama, quite a young man, who proffered hospitality for the next few days among his friends, inns having ceased. The thought of " poisoned feasts " never crossed my mind!

The greater part of the bizarre population of the quaint mountain town escorted us to the gateway. Superb weather favored our departure. The heat of the sun melted the snows towards midday, adding volume to the thunderous roll of the Siao Ho, above which, after descending to the water's edge, the bridle-track is carried over spurs and abutments of limestone. There is a decided change in the scenery. The river, no longer closely hemmed in by the walls of a tremendous cleft, is broader and stiller; there are shingle banks and stretches of cultivated land, and it cuts its way through the ranges instead of following their clefts. A marked feature of the Siao Ho is the extraordinarily abrupt bends which it makes, and that at most of these a sugar-loaf peak, forest-clothed below, and naked rock above, rises sheer from the river-bed, possibly to a height of from 2000 to 3000 feet. Great opening allow of inspiring views of high, conical, snow-clothed peaks, heavily timbered below the snow; one group, called by the Chinese "The Throne of Snow", consisting of a Great central peak, with nine others of irregular altitudes surrounding it.

Climb the Peh-teo-shan spur by a long series of rocky, broken zigzags, cut on its side through a hazel wood, and reaching an altitude of about 9270 feet in advance of my men, I felt the joy of a "born traveler" as I watched the mules with their picturesque Man-tze muleteer, the eleven men no longer staggering under burdens, but jumping, laughing, and singing, some of them with leaves of an artemisia stuffed into their nostrils to prevent the bleeding from the nose which had trouble them since leaving Weichou, the two soldiers in their rags, and myself the worst ragamuffin of all. There were many such elysian moments in this grand "Beyond".

The summit is thick with poles, some of them bearing flags inscribed in Tibetan characters in honor of the Spirit of the Pass, and there is a large cairn, to which my men added their quota of stones. Fifteen or sixteen hundred feet below, the river looks like a green silk cord interwoven with silver. There is a sharp bend and a widening, from which rise two conical peaks, forest-clothed and craggy. Lateral gorges run up from the river, walked in by high, frowning, forest-covered mountains, breaking into grey, bare peaks, and crags gleaming in the sunshine. To the north-west the canyon broadens. Mountains rise above mountains, forest-covered, except where their bare ribs and buttress stand harshly out above the greenery, and above them great, sunlit, white clouds were massed, emphasizing the blue gloom of pines; and far higher, raised by an atmospheric effect to an altitude which no mountains of this earth attain to, in the full sunshine of a glorious day, were three illuminated snow-peaks, whose height from the green and silver river, judged by the eye alone, might have been 30000 feet! They might have been "the mountains of the land which is very far off," for the lighted clouds below separated them from all other earthly things, and their dazzling summits are unprofaned by the foot of man.

——**Excerpted from *The Yangtze Valley and Beyond*. 1899:404 - 407. London:John Murray.**

New Words and Expressions

scanty [ˈskænti]adj. 缺乏的;吝啬的;仅有的;稀疏的
canyon [ˈkænjən]n. 峡谷
deluge [ˈdeljuːdʒ]n. 洪水;泛滥;暴雨 vt. 使泛滥;压倒
officialism [əˈfiʃəlizəm]n. 官场;官员;官僚作风
muleteer [ˌmjuːləˈtiə(r)]n. 赶骡人
proffer [ˈprɒfə]n. 提供;提出;提议 vt. 提供;提出;奉献
quaint [kweint]adj. 古雅的;奇怪的;离奇有趣的
abutment [əˈbʌtmənt]n. 邻接;接界;桥墩
hem [hem]n. 边;边缘;摺边 vt. 包围;给……缝边
shingle [ˈʃiŋg(ə)l]n. 墙面板;木瓦 vt. 用盖板覆盖

cleft [kleft]adj. 分裂的；劈开的 n. 裂缝；龟裂
timber ['timbə]n. 木材；木料
artemisia [ˌɑːti'miziə]n. 蒿属；艾草
nostril ['nɒstr(ə)l]n. 鼻孔
lateral ['lætərəl]adj. 侧面的；横向的 n. 侧部
frown [fraʊn]vi. 皱眉；不同意 vt. 皱眉；蹙额

Episode Ⅳ

Into her archaic and unreformed Orientalism, the Western leaven has fallen for good or evil. Rudely awakened by the Japanese victories out of her long sleep, China, half dismayed and wholly dazed, with much loss of "face," and shaken confidence in the methods of diplomacy which have served her so well in the past, finds herself confronted by an array of powerful, grasping, ambitious, and not always over-scrupulous powerful, bent, it may be, on over-reaching her and each other, ringing with barbarian hands the knell of the customs and polity which are the legacy of Confucius, clamouring for ports and concessions, and bewildering her with reforms, suggestions, and demands, of which she sees neither the expediency nor the necessity.

In this turmoil, and with the European nations thundering at her gates, it is impossible for China to attempt any reforms which would not from the nature of the case be piecemeal and superficial. The reform of an administration like hers needs the prolonged and careful consideration of the best minds in the empire, with such skilled and disinterested foreign advice as was given by Sir Harry Parkes to Japan when she embarked on her new career.

It must be remembered that the remodeling of the administrative system of China is beset with difficulties which have not existed in any other country, and which are accentuated by the vast population and area of the empire. Chinese statesmen (if there be such) have to consider what reforms could be carried out with the approval of the messes, i. e., without bringing about a revolution. The very abuses of administration have gained something of the sanctity which attends on custom among this singular people. It is the most important that those who have to deal with Chinese affairs should be able to obtain such information as would enable them to make a just estimate of the strength and probable diffusion of the desire for reform among the literati, at whose feet the masses lie with a genuine reverence.

China is certainly at the dawn of a new era. Whether the twentieth century shall place her where she ought to be, in the van of Oriental nations, or whether it shall witness her disintegration and decay, depends very largely on the statesmanship and influence of Great Britain.

——Excerpted from *The Yangtze Valley and Beyond*. 1899:543 - 544. London:John Murray.

New Words and Expressions

archaic [ɑːˈkeiik]adj. 古代的;陈旧的;古色古香的
scrupulous [ˈskrupjələs]adj. 细心的;小心谨慎的
knell [nel]n. 丧钟声;凶兆 vi. 鸣丧钟;预报凶兆
clamour [ˈklæmə]vt. 吵闹 vi. 叫喊;大声地要求 n. 喧闹
expediency [ikˈspiːdiənsi]n. 方便;权宜;私利
disinterested [disˈint(ə)ristid]adj. 无私的;公正的;冷漠的
diffusion [diˈfjuːʒ(ə)n]n. 扩散;传播;[光]漫射
van [væn]n. 先锋;厢式货车 vt. 用车搬运

三、思考题

1. 你如何理解《扬子江流域及以外地区》是向世界“传达了这个国家(中国)及其人民的真实印象?”

2. 体会文本中对中国风景尤其是长江三峡和川藏地区的壮丽风光描写的语言特点。

第十二章

远东漫游

一、作品导读

巴尔福(Frederic Henry Balfour,1846—1909),1870 年来到中国经营丝绸、茶叶生意,后来在中国从事新闻和出版事业,先后担任《通闻西报》《华洋通闻》《字林西报》等刊物的主笔,还担任过上海英文报纸《晚报》(1873 年创刊,由柯泰洋行发行)的主编。巴尔福熟悉中国文化、历史与政治,曾翻译过《太上感应篇》《清静经》《阴符经》等道教经典作品,并于 1881 年在伦敦出版《南华真经》(即《庄子》),1884 年在上海出版英文的《道教经典》。巴尔福的代表性著作有《远东漫游》《中国拾零》等。

《远东漫游》一书不同于晚清时期其他西方来华作者撰写的游记,其他作者主要记录在中国各地旅行的所见所闻,而这是一本涉及 19 世纪中叶清朝政治、经济、文化、外交、宗教等方面的"笔游",重在以思维带来的空间移动与想象的"虚拟旅行",这一点类似于中世纪时"座椅上的旅行家"曼德维尔写的《曼德维尔游记》。全书一共 20 章,以中国为主线贯穿全书,涉及中国历史、文化、军事、宗教,以及中国与周边邻国(尤其是日本)之间的关系,同时也简单介绍了中国与英美等国之间的关系。

《远东漫游》总体上以近乎中立的立场,准确、客观地描述了当时中国的文化传统与地位。该书以当时西方一些党派从不同的政治角度出发看待中国的两种极端说法——"恐惧与无限赞美"开篇,前一种说法是"反华派"的观点,认为中国是令人感到"恐惧"的以"中国皇帝"为当权者实施的极权统治,如果把中国理解为众多国家中的一员,这个国家就不存在了;后一种观点是"保华派"的观点,认为中国是一个伟大的、令人羡慕的,甚至是令人敬佩的民族,是少数几个商人自私与野蛮攻击的牺牲品。接着巴尔福为读者介绍他所在的“大清帝国”的情况，中国民间秘密团体的政治意义以及对中国政治的影响，中国的军备，中国与邻国日本的关系，等等。

《远东漫游》一书尤其可贵的是，巴尔福在用笔漫游考察 19 世纪中叶清朝社会各个方面的同时，深入剖析了种种现象中的深层因素。如在《中国军备》一章中他认为中国士兵虽然擅长防御工事，但是不会使用现代武器，这是中国士兵素质低下最突出的体现，导致有时在战争装备强过对手时也每战失败，为理解当时清朝政府在对外战争中屡战屡败提供了新的解释。又如在《中国人看外国文化》一章中，巴尔福分析了当时中国人在接受西方现代科技文化时的思想碰撞，既承认西方造船、造军火等技术高明，但是又对西方的政治与宗教则基本持抵触的态度。可以说，作者对当时中国状况的很多精辟的剖析对当代中国依然有参考价值。

二、作品选读

Episode Ⅰ

Of course the Chinese troops are numerous, but the spell of Oriental multitudes has been broken long ago, and we need not be told that numbers are often an absolute hindrance when the discipline is slack, and the commissariat deficient. We are not prepared to deny that when well led the Imperial troops have ere now conducted themselves bravely before the enemy, but this was when they were convinced of the perfection of their own arms and tactics, and had not been rudely undeceived by finding themselves beaten by Western weapons and Western strategy. Now, everything has been broken down. The prestige of invincibility has been shaken. Like David they are asked to go out against a formidable Goliath, inarmour they have "not proved" and hence they would be uncertain in their movements, difficult to handle, and easily stricken with panic. Their fire-arms would in all probability play them false in the first engagement.

Those troops who had their drill fresh in mind would be obedient and steady; but the men who had forgotten or imperfectly learnt would blunder, hesitate, and throw everything into confusion.

Again, it is utterly impossible to arrive at the numerical strength of the Chinese standing army: we can only say that the mandarins receive pay for the maintenance of about ten times the number of soldiers that actually exist. The Chinese soldier is not only dirty, ill-armed, lazy, and unpractical, but he has not the remotest notion of how to handle even such a rifle as is handed out to him—much less of keeping it clean; while the weapons provided for his use are infinitely more dangerous to himself than to the man he shoots at, and are dear to the Government at seventy-five cents a piece. In fact the Chinese Government is being universally "stuck" in its purchase of both fire-arms and gunboats, and as long as the soldiers are provided with rifles which will explode, and with gunpowder which won't, so long will the army be an utterly useless institution. Then as to military discipline, properly so called, such a thing does not exist. Eighteen hundred men out of two thousand are mere coolies; while as for native drill! Picturesque it may be, but grotesque is no adequate expression for it. Some time ago a "water-drill" took place among a contingent of the soldiery at Ningpo; a performance, which albeit intended for the delectation of His Excellency the Fu-t'ai, seems to have reached the Ultima Thule of absurdity. The manoeuvres of the soldiers reminded one more of the cow-like gambols of Miss Tilly Slowboy than of a formal military review held in the presence of a provincial magnate. They danced and capered about in a fashion as useless as it was insane; they brandished their clumsy swords, and "flashed" their ponderous shields, and yelled like lunatics. Then, encouraged by the martial sounds of a lugubrious ram's-horn, they slipped gingerly into the river, having first provided themselves with life-belts, and then gravely paddled about. Here they remained, marching in line, describing circles, fronting cross-lines in the shape of the letter X, letting off crackers and burnstone, flourishing staves, and hooting for all the world like owls distraught. And is this farce Chinese warfare? "Of what possible use," remarked a foreign gentleman who witnessed this edifying performance, "they could be, save in duck-shooting, I know not, for they might make capital decoys; "but in a fight, a duck-gun or a good strong fishing-net is all that "would be required to effect their capture."

——**Excerpted from *Waifs and Strays from the Fast East*. 1876: 41 – 42. London: Trubner & Co.; Shang-hai: Kelly & Walsh.**

New Words and Expressions

multitude [ˈmʌltitjuːd]n. 群众;多数
commissariat [ˌkɒmiˈseəriət]n. 粮食;粮食补给;军需部
invincibility [inˌvinsəˈbiləti]n. 无敌;不可战胜
armour [ˈɑːmə]n. 盔甲;装甲;护面
mandarin [ˈmænd(ə)rin]n. 普通话;国语;官话;满清官吏
grotesque [grə(ʊ)ˈtesk]n. 怪异的东西 adj. 奇怪的;可笑的
cooly [ˈkuːli]n. 苦力
contingent [kənˈtindʒ(ə)nt]adj. 偶然发生的 n. 分遣队;偶然事件
albeit [ɔːlˈbiːit]conj. 虽然;即使
delectation [ˌdiːlekˈteiʃ(ə)n]n. 愉快;款待;享受
manoeuvre [məˈnuːvɑ(r)]vi. 调动;演习 vt. 诱使;操纵;耍花招 n. 策略
gambol [ˈgæmb(ə)l]vi. 雀跃;耍闹 n. 雀跃;嬉戏
magnate [ˈmægneit]n. 巨头;大资本家;要人
caper [ˈkeipə]vi. 雀跃 n. 跳跃;雀跃
brandish [ˈbrændiʃ]vt. 挥舞;炫耀 n. 挥舞
lunatic [ˈluːnətik]adj. 疯狂的;愚蠢的 n. 疯子;疯人
lugubrious [lʊˈguːbriəs]adj. 悲哀的;悲惨的
gingerly [ˈdʒindʒəli]adv. 小心翼翼地;慎重地
paddle [ˈpæd(ə)l]n. 划桨 vt. 拌;搅;用桨划 vi. 划桨;戏水;涉水
stave [steiv]n. 狭板;梯级 vt. 延缓;击穿;凿孔于
distraught [diˈstrɔːt]adj. 发狂的;心烦意乱的
farce [fɑːs]n. 闹剧;胡闹;笑剧

edify [ˈedifai]vt. 熏陶；启发；教诲

decoy [ˈdiːkɒi]n. 诱饵；诱骗 vt. 诱骗 vi. 被诱

Episode Ⅱ

But it must, of course, be clear to every candid mind that the policy of the Chinese Government with regard to the importation and growth of opium has nothing whatever to do with the morality of the opium-trade itself. It is often said that while the Government fosters the native cultivation of the plant, it is absurd to charge England with forcing on the Chinese a deleterious drug for the mere sake of a profit to the Indian exchequer; that the occasional protests of the Chinese Government are feeble and insincere at best, and that it would be the height of Quixotism to abandon so valuable a branch of commerce on the bare grounds that many Chinese smoke opium to excess. However undeniable such facts as these may be, the chain of argument into which they are often spun is faulty to a degree. We cannot but consider it proved beyond reasonable doubt that the only objection entertained by the governing body in China to the opium-trade is the enormous amount of foreign influence to which it opens the door; and recognizing the fact that the use of opium has now taken too firm a hold upon the nation to be easily shaken off, it now attempts to supply the demand from the fields of China herself, with a view, in time, to get rid of all dependence upon the imported drug whatever. This is the secret of the Government's so-called opposition to the foreign opium-trade, and it is this, and not the paternal benevolence about which such a maudlin fuss is often made, which lies at the root of the Imperial proclamations upon the subject. But of course we cannot point to such a policy as this as a justification of what is considered by many an immoral trade. If it is immoral to supply the people with an alleged poison, neither the approval nor the disapproval, the honesty nor the insincerity, of that people's Government affects our own position one iota; and any attempt to defend the action of the British Government upon this ground, must inevitably prove a failure.

——**Excerpted from *Waifs and Strays from the Fast East*. 1876:149 - 150. London: Trubner & Co.; Shang-hai: Kelly & Walsh.**

New Words and Expressions

importation [ˌimpɔːˈteiʃən]n. 进口;输入品

opium [ˈəʊpiəm]n. 鸦片;麻醉剂 adj. 鸦片的

deleterious [ˌdeliˈtiəriəs]adj. 有毒的;有害的

exchequer [iksˈtʃekə]n. 财源;国库;财政部

feeble [ˈfiːb(ə)l]adj. 微弱的;无力的;虚弱的;薄弱的

quixotism [ˈkwiksətizəm]n. 不切实际的思想或性格;堂吉诃德式性格

paternal [pəˈtɜːn(ə)l]adj. 父亲的;父亲般的

benevolence [biˈnev(ə)l(ə)ns]n. 仁慈;善行

maudlin [ˈmɔːdlin]adj. 感情脆弱的;容易流泪的 n. 伤感;易流泪

proclamation [prɒkləˈmeiʃn]n. 公告;宣布;宣告

justification [dʒʌstifiˈkeiʃ(ə)n]n. 理由;辩护;认为正当;释罪

iota [ɑiˈəʊtə]n. 极微小;希腊语的第九个字母

Notes

...with a view, in time, to get rid of all dependence upon the imported drug whatever (paragraph 1):本句中的 with a view to 意为"着眼于;考虑到;以……为目的",此处引出目的状语。

如:(1)We have lowered the price with a view to getting more market share.

为了获得更大的市场份额,我们降低了产品价格。

(2)As a matter of fact, most disputes can be settled in a friendly way, with view to developing a long-term relationship.

事实上,本着发展长期关系的意愿,大多数争议都是可以通过友好的方式来加以解决的。

Episode Ⅲ

Between twenty and thirty years ago, a gentleman, who appears modestly to have concealed his name, took the trouble to translate the observations of a travelled Chinaman, who once went so far from home as Java, Batavia, and Singapore. Mr. Wang Ta-hai, the adventurous person referred to, was evidently looked upon by his compatriots as a marvel of learning and experience, for the pamphlet in which he detailed his impressions was honored by no fewer than five prefaces; one by the translator, one by Chow Heo-kung of the Huan-luy College, (an institution we have been utterly unable to identify) another by a literary gentleman named Li-wei, of Peking, a fourth by Liu He-ching, wife's uncle to the author, and a fifth by the gifted traveler himself. From the words of Mr. Liu, we gather that his niece's husband was in many respects a rather eminent man; that in the year 1750 he crossed the seas, and, having acquired high literary honors, published a work on Batavia upon which the Prime Minister, Tsai Wan-kung, passed a very high compliment. The Peking gentleman regrets that his fellow-townsman should have wasted so much talent upon a strange and distant region which had not yet come under the influences of the civilizing doctrines of China; but the collegian's preface is the most characteristic. It is written gracefully and well, and evinces many evidences of culture. The writer deplores the lack of geographical knowledge which existed in his country, and congratulates himself upon the novel information here afforded. "In the time of the Emperor Seuen-tih," he says, "of the Ming Dynasty, (1430) the order for Wang San-pao to proceed towards the Western ocean for the purpose of collecting pearls and precious things, is recorded in the national history: his road lay through An-nan westward, but the chart of that country was concealed by the Superintendent Liu Ta-hea, who had no desire to pass over the sea, by which means the track of the Western ocean remained unknown. Our Government, extensively over spreading all things as the heavens do the earth, has caused its unfathomable favor overwhelmingly to reach the Islands of the Sea; so that all who have blood and breath without exception honor their parents, and even the people of the Great West (meaning Europeans) have thought of bringing their cunning accomplishments to scheme after rewards. Latterly, however, the readiness of the Imperial astronomers to estimate the acquirements of our countrymen in order to promote and employ them is daily more manifest, and people from all parts of the Empire come pressing forwards, soliciting a thorough examination, by which a vast amount of native talent is obtained, without depending on foreign aid. Thus it is that those distant countries have now but few persons to visit and inspect them, and there is not so much as a fairy seated on the leaf of a red lotus to bring us a book from thence. He then goes on to praise the author for his perspicacious and useful work; which, he says, serves to testify that the instructions of their august Dynasty are gracefully wafted over the sea, like the influence of Draco among the stars.

——Excerpted from *Waifs and Strays from the Fast East*. 1876:149-150. London:Trubner & Co.;Shang-hai:Kelly & Walsh.

New Words and Expressions

compatriot [kəm'pætriət]n. 同胞;同国人 adj. 同胞的;同国的
pamphlet ['pæmflit]n. 小册子
literary ['lit(ə)(rə)ri]adj. 文学的;书面的;精通文学的
eminent ['eminənt]adj. 杰出的;有名的;明显的
collegian [kə'li:dʒiən]n. 学院的学生;学院的一员
evince [i'vins]vt. 表明;表示;引起
deplore [di'plɔ:]vt. 谴责;悲悼;哀叹;对……深感遗憾
superintendent [su:p(ə)rin'tend(ə)nt]n. 监督人;主管;指挥者
unfathomable [ʌn'fæð(ə)məb(ə)l]adj. 深不可测的;莫测高深的
solicit [sə'lisit]vt. 征求;招揽;请求;乞求
perspicacious [,pɜ:spi'keiʃəs]adj. 有洞察力的;聪颖的;敏锐的

三、思考题

1.《远东漫游》类似于中世纪时“座椅上的旅行家”曼德维尔写的《曼德维尔游记》，这两部“虚拟的游记”对中国形象的描绘有什么不同？

2. 作者对当时中国状况有很多精辟的剖析，请在文中找出这样的例子。

第十三章

消失的地平线

一、作品导读

詹姆斯·希尔顿(James Hilton,1900—1954),英国著名作家,出生于英国兰开夏郡,卒于美国加利福尼亚。詹姆斯·希尔顿是二战前后享誉英美的畅销书作家,20岁发表小说处女作,33岁成为英国霍桑登文学奖获得者,42岁荣膺奥斯卡最佳剧本奖,代表作《消失的地平线》和《万世师表》被改编成电影。

小说《消失的地平线》的背景是20世纪30年代初——一战后经济危机,二战的风雨也即将来临,当时西方社会正处于一种沮丧、恐慌、动荡不安的状态。人们在对现状不满的同时,希望找到一个保存文明、保存性命的地方,于是詹姆斯·希尔顿在《消失的地平线》中虚构了一个神秘的世外桃源——香格里拉。小说出版后,立刻在欧美引起了轰动,很快风靡世界,并获得霍桑登文学奖。《不列颠文学家辞典》称此书的功绩之一是为英语词汇创造了"Shang-ri-la"一词。

小说中飞机的目的地是雪山环绕的圣境——香格里拉,香格里拉在何处?居住何人?奉行何种理念?历来都是读者和研究者所关注的问题。詹姆斯·希尔顿的过人之处在于创造了"Shang-ri-la"一词并赋予其生命力,他在小说中将香格里拉放置在广袤人稀、荒凉神秘,真实又难以到达的地域——青藏高原。多年来,云南的迪庆、丽江,四川的稻城,克什米尔的拉达克,以及喜马拉雅山周边的许多地区都被人们指认为是香格里拉,但是都有争议。其实小说中的香格里拉并非是现实中某个具体地点,而是一个仿佛在遥远的世外,又似乎在人们旅行的路途中,一个可以无限靠近,却又永远不能抵达的地方。小说中香格里拉的人们信奉天主、弹奏肖邦、使用英语，寺庙领袖——住持佩罗的族属、姓名和出生地也都来自欧罗巴。因此，小说中的香格里拉既不在西方，也不在东方，它在两个世界之间，有人说它是异质的他国，也有人说它是“异乡的本土”，即处在万里之遥的远东的另一个欧洲——“在那东方的西方”。

小说《消失的地平线》的衍生产品有电影、音乐、电子游戏、酒店等。

以下节选的是詹姆斯·希尔顿对高原环境的传神描写，尤其是对雪山和冰峰“理性之美”的理解，以及小说主人公康维为代表的“迷失的一代”的精神诉求。

二、作品选读

Episode Ⅰ

There was enough of the schoolboy still in Mallinson to make him respond to the curt command of a senior, though he was obviously in poor control of himself. Conway, though sorry for him, was more concerned with the immediate problem of the pilot, since he, alone of them all, might be able to give some explanation of their plight. Conway had no desire to discuss the matter further in a merely speculative way; there had been enough of that during the journey. He was uneasy now beyond his continuing mental curiosity, for he was aware that the whole situation had ceased to be excitingly perilous and was threatening to become a trial of endurance ending in catastrophe.

Keeping vigil throughout that gale-tormented night, he faced facts none the less frankly because he did not trouble to enunciate them to the others. He guessed that the flight had progressed far beyond the western range of the Himalaya towards the less known heights of the KuenLun. In that event they would by now have reached the loftiest and least hospitable part of the earth's surface, the Tibetan plateau, two miles high even in its lowest valleys, a vast, uninhabited, and largely unexplored region of windswept upland. Somewhere they were, in that forlorn country, marooned in far less comfort than on most desert islands. Then abruptly, as if to answer his curiosity by increasing it, a rather awe-inspiring change took place. The moon, which he had thought to be hidden by clouds, swung over the lip of some shadowy eminence and, whilst still not showing itself directly, unveiled the darkness ahead. Conway could see the outline of a long valley with rounded, sad-looking low hills on either side, jet-black against the deep electric blue of the night sky. But it was to the head of the valley that his eyes were led irresistibly, for there, soaring into the gap, and magnificent in the full shimmer of moonlight, appeared what he took to be the loveliest mountain on earth. It was an almost perfect cone of snow, simple in outline as if a child had drawn it, and impossible to classify as to size, height, or nearness. It was so radiant, so serenely poised, that he wondered for a moment if it were real at all. Then, while he gazed, a tiny puff clouded the edge of the pyramid, giving life to the vision before the faint rumble of the avalanche confirmed it.

——**Excerpted from *Lost Horizon*. 1933: 49 – 50. West Sussex: James Hilton.**

New Words and Expressions

awe-inspiring [ˈɔːin-spaiəriŋ]adj. 使人敬畏的；令人惊叹的

avalanche [ˈævəlæntʃ]n. 雪崩 vt. 雪崩 vi. 崩塌

catastrophe [kəˈtæstrəfi]n. 大灾难；大祸；惨败

curt [kəːt]adj. 简略的；简要的；草率的

eminence [ˈeminəns]n. 显赫；卓越；高处

enunciate [iˈnʌnsieit]vt. 发音；阐明；宣布 vi. 阐明；清晰地发音

forlorn [fəˈlɔːn]adj. 被遗弃的；绝望的；孤独的

gale-tormented [ˈgeil-ˈtɔː mentid]adj. 狂风大作的

Himalaya [himəˈleiə]喜马拉雅山脉

irresistibly [irəˈzistəbli]adv. 无法抵抗地；不能压制地；极为诱惑人地

jet-black [ˈdʒet-ˈblæk]adj. 黑而发亮的；墨黑的；黑玉色的

maroon [məˈruːn]v. 使孤立 n. 栗色；逃亡黑人奴隶；孤立的人

perilous [ˈperiləs]adj. 危险的；冒险的

plight [plɑit]n. 困境；境况；誓约 vt. 保证；约定

poise [pɔiz]n. 平衡；姿势；镇静 vt. 使平衡 vi. 平衡；准备好；悬着

rumble [ˈrʌmbl]vi. 隆隆作响 n. 隆隆声；抱怨声

serenely [səˈriːnli]adv. 安详地；沉着地；宁静地

shadowy [ˈʃædəʊi]adj. 朦胧的；有阴影的；虚无的；暗黑的

Tibetan plateau [tiˈbetənplætəʊ]青藏高原

vigil [ˈvidʒil]n. 守夜；监视；不眠；警戒

Notes

1. Keeping vigil throughout that gale-tormented night, he faced (Paragraph 2)：这里的“keeping...”是分词独立结构，表示伴随动作。分词独立结构可表示伴随情况、陪衬动作、附加说明以及表示时间、原因、条件等。

如：(1) He ran back to the kitchen, eggs *held* carefully in her hand.

他小心翼翼地拿着鸡蛋，跑回厨房。(伴随动作)

(2)They *being* blind men, how could they see the elephants? (＝As they were blind men...)

他们是盲人，怎么能看见那些大象呢？(表示原因)

2. ...whilst still not showing itself directly (Paragraph 2)：这里的“whilst＝while”，表示然而只是拼法不同，多见于英式英语。

如：He scoffed at others' shortcomings, *whilst* he had many shortcomings of his own.

他讥笑别人的缺点，尽管他本人便有很多不足。

3. But it was to the head of the valley that his eyes were led irresistibly, for(Paragraph 2)：这句是强调句型(部分倒装)，正常语句为 his eyes were led to the head of the valley irresistibly；“for”为连词，引导原因状语从句。

如：(1) I cannot tell whether she is old or young, *for* I have never seen her.

我不知道她年纪多大，因为我从未见过她。

(2) He found it increasingly difficult to read, *for* his eyesight was beginning to fail.

他发觉看书越来越费劲，因为他的视力在下降。

Episode Ⅱ

The night dragged on, as if each minute were something heavy and tangible that had to be pushed to make way for the next. Moonlight faded after a time, and with it that distant spectre of the mountain; then the triple mischiefs of darkness, cold, and wind increased until dawn. As though at its signal, the wind dropped, leaving the world in compassionate quietude. Framed in the pale triangle ahead, the mountain showed again, grey at first, then silver, then pink as the earliest sunrays caught the summit. In the lessening gloom the valley itself took shape, revealing a floor of rock and shingle sloping upwards. It was not a friendly picture, but to Conway, as he surveyed, there came a queer perception of fineness in it, of something that had no romantic appeal at all, but a steely, almost an intellectual quality. The white pyramid in the distance compelled the mind's assent as passionlessly as a Euclidean theorem, and when at last the sun rose into a sky of deep delphinium blue, he felt only a little less than comfortable again.

As the air grew warmer the others wakened, and he suggested carrying the pilot into the open, where the sharp dry air and the sunlight might help to revive him. This was done, and they began a second and pleasanter vigil. Eventually the man opened his eyes and began to speak convulsively. His four passengers stooped over him, listening intently to sounds that were meaningless except to Conway, who occasionally made answers. After some time the man became weaker, talked with increasing difficulty, and finally died. That was about mid-morning.

Conway then turned to his companions. "I'm sorry to say he told me very little – little, I mean, compared with what we should like to know. Merely that we are in Tibet, which is obvious. He didn't give any coherent account of why he had brought us here, but he seemed to know the locality. He spoke a kind of Chinese that I don't understand very well, but I think he said something about a lamasery near here, along the valley I gathered, where we could get food and shelter. Shangri-La, he called it. La is Tibetan for mountain pass. He was most emphatic that we should go there."

——Excerpted from *Lost Horizon*. 1933: 52 – 53. West Sussex: James Hilton.

New Words and Expressions

coherent [kəˈhiər(ə)nt]adj. 连贯的;一致的;清晰的

compassionate [kəmˈpæʃ(ə)nət]adj. 慈悲的;富于同情心的

convulsively [kənˈvʌlsivli]adv. 痉挛性地

delphinium [delˈfiniəm]n. 飞燕草

emphatic [imˈfætik]adj. 着重的;加强语气的;显著的

lamasery [ləˈmɑːs(ə)ri]n. 喇嘛庙

locality [ləˈkæliti]n. 所在;位置;地点

mischief [ˈmistʃif]n. 恶作剧;伤害;顽皮;不和

quietude [ˈkwaiitjuːd]n. 平静;寂静;沉着

shingle [ˈʃiŋg(ə)l]n. 墙面板;木瓦;小招牌

spectre [ˈspektə]n. 幽灵;妖怪;鬼性(等于 specter)

sunray [ˈsʌnrei]n. 紫外线;太阳光线

tangible [ˈtændʒəbl]adj. 有形的;切实的;可触摸的

Notes

1. Framed in the pale triangle ahead, the mountain(Paragraph 1):这

里的“Framed...”是过去分词独立结构，表示方式。过去分词独立结构可表示时间、原因、条件、方式等。

如：(1) Absorbed in the work, he neglected food and sleep.

由于全身心的工作，他废寝忘食。(表示原因)

(2)United, we will be stronger than we are divided.

如果团结，我们就比分裂时更强大。(表示条件)

2. Merely that we are in Tibet, which is obvious(Paragraph 3)：这里的 which 引导非限定性定语，它所引导的非限定性定语从句修饰整个主句(这时被定语从句所修饰的“先行词”要做广义理解)，which 仍在定语从句中作主语、宾语或表语。

如：(1)He set free the birds happily, which was a celebration for his success.

他开心地把鸟放了，这是对他成功的一种庆祝。

(2)Bamboo is hollow, which makes it very light.

竹子是空的，这就使得它很轻。

Episode Ⅲ

To Conway, seeing it first, it might have been a vision fluttering out of that solitary rhythm in which lack of oxygen had encompassed all his faculties. It was, indeed, a strange and half-incredible sight. A group of colored pavilions clung to the mountainside with none of the grim deliberation of a Rhineland castle, but rather with the chance delicacy of flower petals impaled upon a crag. It was superb and exquisite. An austere emotion carried the eye upward from milk-blue roofs to the grey rock bastion above, tremendous as the Wetterhorn above Grindelwald. Beyond that, in a dazzling pyramid, soared the snow slopes of Karakal. It might well be, Conway thought, the most terrifying mountainscape in the world, and he imagined the immense stress of snow and glacier against which the rock functioned as a gigantic retaining wall. Someday, perhaps, the whole mountain would split, and a half of Karakal's icy splendor come toppling into the valley. He wondered if the slightness of the risk combined with its fearfulness might even be found agreeably stimulating. Hardly less an enticement was the downward prospect, for the mountain wall continued to drop, nearly perpendicularly, into a cleft that could only have been the result of some cataclysm in the far past. The floor of the valley, hazily distant, welcomed the eye with greenness; sheltered from winds, and surveyed rather than dominated by the lamasery, it looked to Conway a delightfully favored place, though if it were inhabited its community must be completely isolated by the lofty and sheerly unscalable ranges on the further side. Only to the lamasery did there appear to be any climbable egress at all. Conway experienced, as he gazed, a slight tightening of apprehension; Mallinson's misgivings were not, perhaps, to be wholly disregarded. But the feeling was only momentary, and soon merged in the deeper sensation, half-mystical, half-visual, of having reached at last some place that was an end, a finality.

——Excerpted from *Lost Horizon*. 1933: 65 – 66. West Sussex: James Hilton.

New Words and Expressions

austere [ɔ'stir]adj. 严峻的；简朴的；苦行的；无装饰的

bastion ['bæstiən]n. 堡垒；棱堡

cataclysm ['kætə, kliz(ə)m]n. 灾难；大洪水，地震；(社会政治的)大变动

cleft [kleft]adj. 分裂的；劈开的 n. 裂缝；龟裂

crag [kræg]n. 峭壁；岩石碎块

egress ['i:gres]n. 外出；出口 vi. 外出

encompass [in'kʌmpəs]vt. 包含；包围；环绕

enticement [in'taismənt]n. 诱惑；怂恿；引诱物；吸引力

finality [fai'næləti]n. 定局；终结；结尾

flutter ['flʌtə]vi. 飘动 vt. 拍；使焦急；使飘动 n. 摆动

grim [grim]adj. 冷酷的；糟糕的；残忍的

impale [im'peil]vt. 刺穿；钉住；使绝望

perpendicularly [pə:pən'dikjuləli]adv. 垂直地；直立地

petal ['pet(ə)l]n. 花瓣

solitary ['sɒlit(ə)ri]adj. 孤独的；独居的 n. 独居者；隐士

splendour ['splendə]n. 显赫（等于 splendor）；光彩壮丽

topple ['tɒp(ə)l]vi. 倾倒；倒塌；摇摇欲坠 vt. 推翻；颠覆

unscalable [ʌn'skeiləb(ə)l]adj. 不能攀登的

Notes

1. Beyond that, in a dazzling pyramid, soared the snow slopes of Karakal. 在叙述和描写性的句子中，有时为了加强语气，可把表示地点的介词短语放在句首。如果句子的主要动词是不及物动词，要改变句子的词序，把动词移到主语的前面。注意：如果句子的动词是系动词或及物动词，则不可倒装。

如：(1) In the garden everything *is* peaceful.

花园里一切都是静悄悄的。

(2) Through the windows he *could see* his kids playing football in the garden.

透过窗户，他看见孩子们在花园里踢足球。

2. Only to the lamasery did there appear to be any climbable egress at all. 此句为倒装句，自然语序为 There appeared to be any climbable egress at all only to the lamasery.

英语句子的结构一般是"主语 ＋ 谓语"，语法上称这种语序为自然语序。但有时出于语法结构的需要或修辞的需要，常把句子中的一部分或全部倒转过来，这种语序就是倒装语序。按照英语语法规则，"only＋状语"位于句首，句子通常要用倒装语序。

如：(1) Only then did I realize that I was wrong.

只是到了那时我才意识到是我错了。

(2) Only by shouting was he able to make himself heard.

他只有叫喊才能让别人听到他。

(3) Only by working hard can you succeed.

只有努力工作你才能成功。

三、思考题

1. 詹姆斯·希尔顿心中的香格里拉是一个怎样的世界？

2. 詹姆斯·希尔顿在文中是怎样表达对雪山和冰峰“理性之美”的理解？

3. 小说主人公康维为代表的“迷失的一代”的精神诉求的背景是什么？

第十四章

西行漫记

一、作品导读

埃德加·斯诺(Edgar Snow,1905—1972),美国著名记者。斯诺1928年来到中国,曾任欧美几家报社驻华记者、通讯员,还兼任过北平燕京大学(今北京大学)新闻系讲师(1933—1935)。斯诺喜欢到处旅行,到中国后干的第一件差事是乘火车四处旅行,为中国旅行社和铁路部门撰写旅游指南,在中国他先后定期为《纽约先驱论坛》《星期六晚邮报》等杂志写稿。著作有《西行漫记》《远东前线》《活的中国》等11部。

埃德加·斯诺毕生致力中美友好交往,也是美国的中国问题专家,他与艾格尼丝·史沫特莱、安娜·路易斯·斯特朗(即3S,因三人英文名字第一个字母均为S)并称为中国人民的三位亲密好朋友。中华人民共和国成立后,斯诺分别在1960年、1964年、1970年对中国进行了三次长期访问。1970年10月1日毛泽东和斯诺在天安门城楼上亲切交谈时,毛泽东高度评价他说"我没有变,你也没有变"。

《西行漫记》(又译《红星照耀中国》)是斯诺1936年6月到10月去陕北旅行的采访纪实,是他在"红色中国"4个月所见、所闻、所思、所感的结晶。《西行漫记》以史诗般的手法对"红色中国"进行了全面具体、丰富翔实的报道,全书结构组织合理、叙事明白清晰、描写生动活泼、人物形象生动、细节捕捉细腻,最令人信服的是斯诺在书中预测了中国社会革命运动的未来,历史证明他的预测是正确的。

《西行漫记》自1937年英文版问世、1938年中译本出版至今经久不衰,被誉为是"每一页都是有意义的""是一部经典著作""标志着西方了解中国的新纪元"的作品。斯诺的《西行漫记》和他的《前西行漫记》(原名《外国记者西北印象》)、尼姆·威尔斯的《续西行漫记》(又译《红色中国内幕》)、哈里森·福尔曼的《北行漫记》(又译《红色中国报道》)都是报道当时"红色中国"的作品。

二、作品选读

Episode Ⅰ

During my seven years in China, hundreds of questions had been asked about the Chinese Red Army, the Soviets, and the Communist movement. Eager partisans could supply you with a stock of ready answers, but these remained highly unsatisfactory. How did they know? They had never been to Red China.

The fact was that there had been perhaps no greater mystery among nations, no more confused an epic, than the story of Red China. Fighting in the very heart of the most populous nation on earth, the Celestial Reds had for nine years been isolated by a news blockade as effective as a stone fortress. A wall of thousands of enemy troops constantly surrounded them; their territory was more inaccessible than Tibet. No one had voluntarily penetrated that wall and returned to write of his experiences since the first Chinese soviet was established in southeastern Hunan, in November, 1927.

Even the simplest points were disputed. Some people denied that there was such a thing as a Red Army. There were only thousands of hungry brigands. Some denied even the existence of soviets. They were an invention of Communist propaganda. Yet Red sympathizers extolled both as the only salvation for all the ills of China. In the midst of this propaganda and counterpropaganda, credible evidence was lacking for dispassionate observers seeking the truth. Here are some of the unanswered questions that interested everyone concerned with politics and the quickening history of the Orient.

Was or was not this Red Army of China a mass of conscious Marxist revolutionaries, disciplined by and adhering to a centralized program and a unified command under the Chinese Communist Party? If so, what was that program? The Communists claimed to be fighting for agrarian revolution, and against imperialism, and for soviet democracy and national emancipation. Nanking said that the Reds were only a new type of vandals and marauders led by "intellectual bandits". Who was right? Or was either one?

Before 1927, members of the Communist Party were admitted to the Kuomintang, but in April of that year there began a great "purgation". Communists, as well as unorganized radical intellectuals and thousands of organized workers and peasants, were executed on an extensive scale under Chiang Kai-shek, the Right-wing leader, which seized power, to form a "National Government" at Nanking. Since then it had been a crime punishable by death to be a Communist or a Communist sympathizer, and thousands had paid that penalty. Yet thousands more continued to run the risk. Thousands of peasants, workers, students, and soldiers joined the Red Army in armed struggle against the military dictatorship of the Nanking regime. Why? What inexorable force drove them on to support suicidal political opinions? What were the fundamental quarrels between the Kuomintang and the Kungch'antang?

What were the Chinese Communists like? In what way did they resemble, in what way were they unlike, Communists or Socialists elsewhere? The tourists asked if they wore long beards, made noises with their soup, and carried homemade bombs in their briefcases. The serious-minded wanted to know whether they were "genuine" Marxists. Did they read Capital and the works of Lenin? Had they a thoroughly Socialist economic program? Were they Stalinites or Trotskyites? Or neither? Was their movement really an organic part of the World Revolution? Were they true inter-nationalists? "Mere tools of Moscow", or primarily nationalists struggling for an independent China?

——**Excerpted from *Red Star Over China*. 1938:455 – 466. New York: Random House, Inc.**

New Words and Expressions

partisan [ˈpɑːtizæn]n. 游击队;虔诚信徒;党羽
epic [ˈepik]n. 史诗;叙事诗;史诗般的作品
celestial [siˈlestiəl]adj. 天上的;天空的 n. 神仙;天堂里的居民
blockade [bləˈkeid]vt. 封锁 n. 阻塞
fortress [ˈfɔːtris]n. 堡垒;要塞 vt. 筑要塞;以要塞防守
inaccessible [inəkˈsesib(ə)l]adj. 难达到的;难接近的;难见到的
brigand [ˈbrigənd]n. 强盗;土匪;盗贼
propaganda [prɔpəˈgændə]n. 宣传;传道总会
extol [ikˈstəul]vt. 颂扬;赞美;赞颂
salvation [sælˈveiʃ(ə)n]n. 拯救;救助
counterpropaganda [ˈkauntə, prɒpəˈgændə]n. 反宣传
dispassionate [disˈpæʃənət]adj. 不带感情的;平心静气的;公平的
centralize [ˈsɛntrəlaiz]vt. 使集中;使成为……的中心;使集权
agrarian [əˈgreəriən]adj. 土地的;耕地的;有关土地的
vandal [ˈvændl]n. 文化艺术的破坏者;蓄意破坏者
marauder n. 掠夺者;抢劫者;猛虎
bandit [ˈbændit]n. 强盗;土匪;恶棍;敲诈者
purgation [pɜːˈgeiʃ(ə)n]n. 清洗;洗罪;(吃泻药)通便
dictatorship [dikˈteitəʃip]n. 专政;独裁权;独裁者职位
Kuomintang [ˈkwəuminˈtæŋ]n. 国民党
inexorable [inˈeks(ə)rəb(ə)l]adj. 无情的;不屈不挠的;不可阻挡的;无法改变的
suicidal [s(j)uːiˈsaid(ə)l]adj. 自杀的;自杀性的;自取灭亡的
serious-minded [ˈsiəriəsˈmaindid]adj. 认真的

Notes

1. ...no more confused an epic, than the story of Red China. Fighting in the very heart of the most populous nation on earth (Paragraph 2): "no more...than"表示对两者都否定，意为"同……一样不"(=neither...nor...)。

如:(1) He is no more a writer than a painter.

他既不是画家，也不是作家。(=He is neither a painter nor a writer.)

(2)He's no more able to read Spanish than I am.

他和我都读不懂西班牙语。

2. In the midst of this propaganda and counterpropaganda, credible evidence was lacking for dispassionate observers seeking the truth (Paragraph 2): "in the midst of..."意为"在……之中"。

如:(1)In the midst of our family tragedy, I made a peculiar discovery.

在我们家庭的悲剧中，我发现了一个特殊的现象。

(2)In the midst of this, man seems so trivial.

在这个整体中，人类显得是如此的卑微。

Episode Ⅱ

On July 16, 1936, I sat on a square, backless stool inside Mao Tse-tung's residence. It was after nine at night, "Taps" had been sounded and nearly all lights were out. The walls and ceiling of Mao's home were of solid rock; beneath was a flooring of bricks. Cotton gauze extended halfway up windows also hollowed from stone, and candles sputtered on the square, unpainted table before us, spread with a clean red-felt cloth. Mrs. Mao was in an adjoining room making compote from wild peaches purchased that day from a fruit merchant. Mao sat with his legs crossed, in a deep shelf hewn from the solid rock, and smoked a Chien Men cigarette.

Seated next to me was Wu Liang-ping, a young soviet "functionary" who acted as interpreter in my "formal" interviews with Mao Tse-tung. I wrote down in full in English Mao Tse-tung's answers to my questions, and these were then translated into Chinese and corrected by Mao, who is noted for his insistence upon accuracy of detail. With the assistance of Mr. Wu, the interviews were retranslated into English, and because of such precautions I believe these pages to contain few errors of reporting. They were, of course, the strictly partisan views of the leader of the Chinese Communists views being made known to the Western world for the first time.

Wu Liang-ping, to whom I am indebted for much assistance in gathering material, was the son of a rich landlord in Fenghua, Chiang Kaishek's native district in Chekiang. He had fled from there some years ago when his father, apparently an ambitious burgher, wished to betroth him to a relative of the Generalissimo. Wu was a graduate of Ta Hsia University, in Shanghai. There Patrick Givens, chief of the Criminal Investigation Department of the British-controlled police of the International Settlement, had arrested Wu Liang-ping. Charged with Communist activity, Wu spent two years in the Settlement's Ward Road Jail. He had studied in France, England, and Russia, was twenty-six years old, and for his energetic labors as a Communist received his uniform, room, and food—the latter consisting chiefly of millet and noodles.

Mao began to answer my first question, about Communist policy toward Japan, which was this: "If Japan is defeated and driven from China, do you think that the major problem of 'foreign imperialism' will in general have been solved here?"

"Yes. If other imperialist countries do not act like Japan, and if China defeats Japan, it will mean that the Chinese masses have awakened, have mobilized, and have established their independence. Therefore the main problem of imperialism will have been solved."

"Under what conditions do you think the Chinese people can exhaust and defeat the forces of Japan?" I asked.

He replied: "Three conditions will guarantee our success: first, the achievement of the National United Front against Japanese imperialism in China; second, the formation of a World Anti-Japanese United Front; third, revolutionary action by the oppressed peoples at present suffering under Japanese imperialism. Of these, the central necessity is the union of the Chinese people themselves."

...

It was past two o'clock in the morning and I was exhausted, but I could see no signs of fatigue on Mao's thoughtful face. He alternately walked up and down between the two little rooms, sat down, lay down, leaned on the table, and read from a sheaf of reports in the intervals when Wu translated and I wrote. Mrs. Mao also was still awake. Suddenly both of them bent over and gave an exclamation of delight at a moth that had languished beside the candle. It was a really lovely thing, with wings shaded a delicate apple-green and fringed in a soft rainbow of saffron and rose. Mao opened a book and pressed this gossamer of color between its leaves.

Could such people really be thinking seriously of war?

——Excerpted from *Red Star Over China*. 1938: 455 - 466. New York: Random House, Inc.

New Words and Expressions

gauze [gɔːz]n. 纱布;薄纱;薄雾

hollow [ˈhɒləʊ]adj. 空的;中空的 vt. 使成为空洞

sputter [ˈspʌtə]vi. 发噼啪声;唾沫飞溅 vt. 飞溅出;喷出

adjoin [əˈdʒɔin]vi. 毗连;邻接; vt. 毗连;邻接

compote [ˈkɒmpəʊt]n. 煮熟的糖渍水果;高脚果盘

hewn [hjʊn]vt. 砍(hew 的过去分词)adj. 粗削的

burgher [ˈbɜːgə]n. 市民(现主要指某些欧洲国家中产阶级的市民或镇民)

betroth [biˈtrəʊð]vt. 同……订婚;许配

millet [ˈmilit]n. 小米;粟;稷;黍的籽实

mobilize [ˈməʊbəlaiz]vt. 动员;调动;集合;使……松动

sheaf [ʃiːf]n. 捆;束;扎 vt. 捆;束;扎

exclamation [ˌekskləˈmeiʃ(ə)n]n. 感叹;惊叫;惊叹词

moth [mɒθ]n. 蛾;蛀虫

languish [ˈlæŋgwiʃ]vi. 憔悴;凋萎;失去活力;苦思

fringe [frindʒ]n. 边缘；穗；刘海 adj. 边缘的；附加的 vt. 加穗于

saffron [ˈsæfr(ə)n]n. 藏红花；橙黄色 adj. 藏红花色的；橘黄色的

gossamer [ˈɡɒsəmə]n. 蛛丝；薄纱；小蜘蛛网 adj. 轻飘飘的；薄弱的

International Settlement n. 国际清算

Criminal Investigation Department n. 刑事调查局

Notes

Seated next to me was Wu Liang-ping, a young soviet "functionary" who acted as interpreter in my "formal" interviews with MaoTse-tung (paragraph 2)：这里的"Seated..."是过去分词独立结构，表示伴随方式。

如：(1) Inspired by his example, hundreds of others volunteered to join us.
在他的带动下，成百上千的人都志愿参加了我们的工作。

(2) Encouraged by Mr. Fu, I checked on the machine's operation record.
在傅老师的鼓励下，我查看了一下机器的操作记录。

Episode Ⅲ

There was an accomplished social scientist named Lenin. "History generally," he wrote, "and the history of revolutions in particular, is always richer in content, more varied, more many-sided, more lively and 'subtle', than the best parties and the most class-conscious vanguards of the most advanced class imagine. This is understandable, because the best vanguards express the class consciousness, the will, the passion, the fantasy of tens of thousands, while the revolution is made, at the moment of its climax and exertion of all human capabilities, by the class consciousness, the will, the passion, and the fantasy of tens of millions who are urged on by the very acutest class struggle." In what ways had Chinese history proved richer in content, more varied, more many-sided, more lively and "subtle" than the Communist theoreticians foresaw a decade or so ago? To be specific, why had the Red Army failed to win power in China? In attempting an answer one had to recall again, and keep clearly in mind, the Communist conception of the Chinese revolution, and of its main objectives.

...

And that, I believed, was the contour of the Communist picture of the future as China waited for Japan to strike. One might not follow all of it, but this at least seemed certain—that what Lenin had written more than twenty years before was still true: "Whatever may be the fate of the great Chinese revolution, against which various 'civilized' hyenas are now sharpening their teeth, no forces in the world will restore the old serfdom in Asia, nor erase from the face of the earth the heroic democracy of the popular masses in the Asiatic and semi-Asiatic countries."

And another thing seemed equally certain. Neither could the democratic Socialist ideas for which tens of thousands of youths had already died in China, nor the energies behind them, be destroyed. The movement for social revolution in China might suffer defeats, might temporarily retreat, might for a time seem to languish, might make wide changes in tactics to fit immediate necessities and aims, might even for a period be submerged, be forced underground, but it would not only continue to mature; in one mutation or another it would eventually win, simply because (as this book proves, if it proves anything) the basic conditions which had given it birth carried within themselves the dynamic necessity for its triumph.

——Excerpted from *Red Star Over China*. 1938: 455 – 466. New York: Random House, Inc.

New Words and Expressions

vanguard [ˈvængɑːd]n. 先锋;前锋;科学卫星

contour [ˈkɒntʊə]n. 轮廓;概要 vt. 画轮廓;画等高线

hyena [haiˈiːnə]n. 鬣狗;土狼

serfdom [ˈsəːfdəm]n. 农奴境遇;农奴身份

submerge [səbˈmɜːdʒ]vt. 淹没;把……浸入;沉浸 vi. 淹没;潜入水中;湮没

mutation [mjuːˈteiʃ(ə)n]n. [遗] 突变;变化;元音变化

Notes

Neither could the democratic Socialist ideas for which tens of thousands of youths had already died in China, nor the energies behind them, be destroyed (paragraph 4):这里的"neither...nor..."表示"既不……也不……",其含义是否定的,可连接任意两个并列的成分(词语或句子)。

如:(1) Neither dad nor mum is at home today.

今天父母都不在家。

(2)The novel is neither realistic nor poetic.

那部小说既不写实,也没有诗意。

三、思考题

1. 你如何理解斯诺对中国社会革命运动前景的预测?
2. 《西行漫记》的艺术魅力在哪些地方有突出的体现?

后　记

2015年，我有幸被国家旅游局选拔为“2015年旅游业青年专家培养计划人选”。结合自己近几年关注的旅行跨文化研究领域，我以“晚清时期西方旅行文学的中国形象研究”（课题批准号：TYETP201550）为题开展研究，但实际的研究有所变化：首先，考虑到“西方旅行文学的中国形象”这一课题在时间跨度上的完整性，超越了原来的晚清时期追溯到蒙元时代，即所选择的作品从13世纪末《马可波罗游记》到20世纪30年代的《西行漫记》；其次，考虑到成果最终能更多分享给旅游院校、外国文学专业和相关专业的学生，成果形式由原来的专著变为教材形式，并由桂林旅游学院外国语学院2015级旅游英语专业本科学生最早使用；再次，考虑到增加了工作量，我邀请了桂林旅游学院外国语学院的江利华副教授和厦门医学院外语教研部副教授钟俊博士加入，成果变成三人合作完成。尽管有以上变化，本教材仍然作为本人“2015年旅游业青年专家培养计划人选”结题成果之一。

本教材编写的工作任务根据三人专长而定。本人对旅游基础理论研究、旅行跨文化领域比较感兴趣，著有《旅游表演学》（南开大学出版社，2015年）等；江利华副教授曾赴加拿大访学，译作有《一臂之间：美国总统保镖回忆录》（广西师范大学出版社，2016年）、《念大学会有回报吗？——美国高等教育之现状》（广西师范大学出版社，2017年），同时也担任旅游英语本科专业的课程教学，在翻译和英语教学方面积累了丰富的经验；钟俊于2015年在厦门大学外文学院获得文学博士学位，研究方向为双语词典与翻译研究，在国内外期刊发表学术论文20余篇，现担任厦门医学院外语教研部主任。具体工作任务如下：朱江勇（负责文本确定、作品导读撰写、章节节选、前言、后记）；江利华（负责部分章节节选、思考题、教材完善）；钟俊（负责注释和词汇部分）。

本教材编写过程中得到诸多单位、同仁的关心与帮助！首先，感谢国家旅游局将我纳入“2015年旅游业青年专家培养计划人选”，感谢本期计划人选的“班主任”——国家旅游局人事司副司长余昌国先生，以及本期计划人选的各位同仁；其次，感谢与我一起编选本教材的两位编者江利华副教授和钟俊博士，感谢为本课题指导的周其厚教授、黄晓萍教授和为本书写序的陈毅平教授，以及为本教材提供外文版资料和修改文稿的涂运根博士、陆礼春博士、彭金玲副教授、翟青青老师！最后，感谢出版本教材的合肥工业大学出版社的各位老师！

由于时间仓促和我们的学识水平有限，本教材存在的不足之处在所难免，希望广大专家学者、读者批评指正！

朱江勇

2018 年 2 月 3 日

于桂林旅游学院